Preschool-Wide Evaluation Tool™

PreSET™

Manual

RESEARCH EDITION

Preschool-Wide Evaluation Tool™
PreSET™
Manual
RESEARCH EDITION

Assessing Universal Program-Wide Positive Behavior Support in Early Childhood

by

Elizabeth A. Steed
Georgia State University
Atlanta

and

Tina M. Pomerleau
Southeastern Regional Education Service Center
Bedford, New Hampshire

·P·A·U·L·H·
BROOKES
PUBLISHING CO®

Baltimore • London • Sydney

Paul H. Brookes Publishing Co.
Post Office Box 10624
Baltimore, Maryland 21285-0624
USA

www.brookespublishing.com

Typeset by Spearhead Global, Inc.
Manufactured in the United States of America by
Victor Graphics, Inc., Baltimore, Maryland.

This manual accompanies the *Preschool-Wide Evaluation Tool™ (PreSET™), Research Edition: An Assessment of Universal Program-Wide Positive Behavior Support in Early Childhood* CD-ROM. To order, contact Paul H. Brookes Publishing Co. (1-800-638-3775; 410-337-9580; www.brookespublishing.com).

The PreSET was developed in part with funding from the Positive Behavioral Interventions and Supports—New Hampshire Initiative, provided by the New Hampshire Department of Education, Bureau of Special Education, Grant 92628, and administered by the New Hampshire Center for Effective Behavioral Interventions and Supports [NH CEBIS], a project of the Southeastern Regional Education Service Center [SERESC] in Bedford, NH.

Library of Congress Cataloging-in-Publication Data
Steed, Elizabeth A.
  Preschool-wide evaluation tool (PreSET) manual : assessing universal program-wide positive behavior support in early childhood / by Elizabeth A. Steed, Georgia State University, Atlanta, and Tina M. Pomerleau, Southeastern Regional Education Service Center, Bedford, New Hampshire. — Research edition.
      p. cm.
  Includes bibliographical references and index.
  ISBN-13: 978-1-59857-207-0
  ISBN-10: 1-59857-207-5
  1. Education, Preschool—United States.   2. Students—Rating of.   I. Pomerleau, Tina M. II. Title.
  LB1140.23.S84 2012
  372.21—dc23   2011039395

British Library Cataloguing in Publication data are available from the British Library.

2016   2015   2014   2013   2012

10   9   8   7   6   5   4   3   2   1

Contents

About the Authors

Elizabeth A. Steed, Ph.D., Assistant Professor and Program Coordinator, Early Childhood Special Education, Department of Educational Psychology and Special Education, Georgia State University, Post Office Box 3979, Atlanta, Georgia 30302

Dr. Steed has more than 15 years of experience working with young children with disabilities and their families in preschool, kindergarten, and home-based settings. She is currently Assistant Professor and Program Coordinator of the Early Childhood Special Education program in the Department of Educational Psychology and Special Education at Georgia State University. Dr. Steed is affiliated faculty in the Center for Leadership in Disability at the University Center for Excellence in Developmental Disabilities at Georgia State University and a faculty partner for their Leadership Education in Neurodevelopmental and Related Disabilities (LEND) program. She is also a member of Georgia's Early Childhood Comprehensive System (ECCS), Georgia Quest for Quality Inclusion, and the Metro Atlanta Preschool Consortium, where she works in collaboration with Georgia's early childhood special educators, administrators, and policy makers. Dr. Steed has been the principal investigator on several research projects focusing on building partnerships with preschool teachers to prevent young children's development of challenging behaviors. She is on the editorial board of *Topics in Early Childhood Special Education*, and her research has been published in peer-reviewed journals and presented at national conferences.

Tina M. Pomerleau, M.Ed., Early Childhood Coordinator, New Hampshire Center for Effective Behavioral Interventions and Supports [NH CEBIS], a project of the Southeastern Regional Education Service Center [SERESC], 29 Commerce Drive, Bedford, New Hampshire 03110

Ms. Pomerleau has more than 10 years of experience working in partnership with early childhood professionals, children, and families in order to effectively address the social and emotional needs of young children with challenging behaviors. Ms. Pomerleau has provided team-based facilitation, individualized consultation, and professional development for the implementation and sustainability of program-wide positive behavior intervention and support (PW-PBIS) within district special education preschool programs, private early childhood programs, and Head Start agencies, focusing on the provision of a three-tiered system of behavioral supports for preschool- and kindergarten-age children. In addition, Ms. Pomerleau also participates in grant writing, research opportunities, and current state and national initiatives including response-to-intervention for the advancement of PW-PBIS in early childhood settings.

Acknowledgments

The *Preschool-Wide Evaluation Tool™ (PreSET™), Research Edition: An Assessment of Universal Program-Wide Positive Behavior Support in Early Childhood* and the *Preschool-Wide Evaluation Tool™ (PreSET™) Manual, Research Edition: Assessing Universal Program-Wide Positive Behavior Support in Early Childhood* were developed with the help of many early childhood professionals and researchers. In addition, special thanks go to Southern New Hampshire Services, Inc. and the Community Action Program Belknap-Merrimack Counties, Inc. Head Start/Early Head Start programs in New Hampshire for their valued contributions. We are grateful to the many individuals who have used the PreSET and provided important feedback throughout the tool's evolution, including Andy Frey, Gerry Morgan, Heather Brey, and Deb Carter. We also thank colleagues from The New Hampshire Center for Effective Behavioral Interventions and Supports [NH CEBIS], including Howard Muscott for providing the opportunity for Tina Pomerleau to participate in the development of the tool, as well as Rebecca Berk, M. Ed., and Valarie Dumont for content they developed and included in the PreSET CD-ROM. We acknowledge the assistance of Mi-Young Webb and Michael Willoughby in data analyses and methodological consultation related to the technical report. Finally, we would like to thank the preschool directors, teachers, and children who welcomed us into their classrooms.

The PreSET was developed, in part, with funding from the Positive Behavioral Interventions and Supports, New Hampshire Initiative, provided by the New Hampshire Department of Education, Bureau of Special Education, Grant 92628, and administered by the New Hampshire Center for Effective Behavioral Interventions and Supports [NH CEBIS], a project of the Southeastern Regional Education Service Center [SERESC] in Bedford, NH.

CHAPTER 1

Introduction to the Preschool-Wide Evaluation Tool

PURPOSE OF THE PreSET

The purpose of the *Preschool-Wide Evaluation Tool™ (PreSET™), Research Edition: An Assessment of Universal Program-Wide Positive Behavior Support in Early Childhood* is to measure an early childhood program's implementation fidelity of program-wide positive behavior intervention and support (PW-PBIS). PW-PBIS is a model of tiered interventions and supports designed to improve young children's social and emotional development and reduce challenging behaviors (Fox & Hemmeter, 2009). The PW-PBIS model was adapted from a model of school-wide positive behavior interventions and support (SW-PBIS) that is utilized in elementary, middle, and high schools. Both models include a focus on data-based decision making, systemwide sustainability features (e.g., establishment of a leadership team, administrative support), and the following three levels of support:

1. Universal interventions for all students

2. Targeted social skills interventions for a small percentage of students who are at risk for social-emotional difficulties

3. Intensive and individualized interventions for a few students who demonstrate chronic and/or severe challenging behavior

SW-PBIS has been implemented in approximately 7,900 schools nationwide (Spaulding, Horner, May, & Vincent, 2008). PW-PBIS has not yet been implemented as widely as SW-PBIS, but its use is growing in preschool classrooms, early childhood programs, and across regional and state systems of early childhood service delivery. Efforts such as the federally funded Technical Assistance Center on Social Emotional Intervention (TACSEI) have increased the visibility of PW-PBIS for early care providers and have provided them with the necessary evidence-based training materials. TACSEI state partners receive special assistance and professional development systems to address young children's social-emotional needs. The Center on the Social and Emotional Foundations for Early Learning (CSEFEL) and the Center for Early Childhood Mental Health Consultation are other examples of funding initiatives that are bringing attention to the issue of young children's social-emotional well-being and providing needed professional development for early childhood educators. National and state policies and funding initiatives are increasingly supporting intervention models such as PW-PBIS that address young children's social-emotional development.

Objective and reliable measures are required to evaluate the impact of PW-PBIS in early childhood settings. The PreSET measures universal and program-wide features of PW-PBIS that are utilized in an early childhood program. The assessment measures the program's implementation of universal practices associated with building positive relationships, supporting children's use of positive social-emotional skills, and preventing challenging behavior in the classroom. The assessment also measures program-wide supports that facilitate adoption and long-term maintenance of PW-PBIS practices, such as administrator support, adequate materials and planning time, and professional development opportunities for teachers. The PreSET measures universal and PW-PBIS features through interviews with the program administrator, teachers in the center, and a sample of children from each classroom, as well as observations of classroom environments and interactions. PreSET results are used to inform educators as they implement PW-PBIS by indicating the features that they are currently implementing well, partially implementing, and not yet implementing. PreSET results may be used from year to year to note progress toward goals and action plan items, as well as to indicate areas that need to be addressed with professional development and/or a revision of program policies.

The PreSET builds upon the framework provided by the School-wide Evaluation Tool (SET; Sugai, Lewis-Palmer, Todd, & Horner, 2001) to evaluate implementation of SW-PBIS in educational environments. The SET includes 28 items organized into seven subscales: Defined Expectations, Expectations Taught, Reward System, Violation System, Monitoring/Evaluation, Management, and District Support. Data are collected for the SET through administrator interviews, teacher and student interviews, classroom observations, and reviews of permanent products. Each administration of the SET by a trained evaluator takes approximately 1–2 hours in a school. Each item of the SET is scored with a value of 0, 1, or 2. Subscale scores may be calculated for each of the seven subscales and a total summary score (an average percent implemented) is reported. The psychometric properties of the SET have been established, and it is used widely as the primary measure of a school's fidelity of implementation of SW-PBIS (Horner et al., 2001; Vincent, Spaulding, & Tobin, 2010).

Although the PreSET abides by the structure and scoring of the SET, items were modified and added so that the instrument would apply to early childhood settings. For example, the Reward System and Violation System subscales on the SET were changed to the Responses to Appropriate and Challenging Behavior subscale on the PreSET to fit the language used in early childhood programs. A Family Involvement subscale was added to the PreSET because of the heavy emphasis on collaboration with families in preschool and early care environments. In addition, the PreSET clarifies that rules and expectations need to be posted in word and visual forms because young children are emergent readers. The PreSET also includes two items concerning the use of supports (e.g., warnings, audiovisual cues) during transitions from one routine to another (e.g., free play to circle) because young children are more likely to exhibit challenging behavior during transitions. In total, the PreSET has 30 items that are organized into eight subscales: Expectations Defined, Behavioral Expectations Taught, Responses to Appropriate and Challenging Behavior, Organized and Predictable Environment, Monitoring and Decision Making, Family Involvement, Management, and Program Support.

POTENTIAL USERS OF THE PreSET

It is assumed that individuals conducting the PreSET have experience and expertise in the following areas: early childhood classroom organization, developmentally appropriate practice, proactive behavior management procedures, assessment of young children, and program evaluation. The intended audience for this manual includes individuals who interact and consult in early childhood settings, such as early childhood behavior consultants, behavior support teachers, inclusion specialists, program administrators, and researchers or evaluators of early childhood positive behavior support.

An outside evaluator (i.e., someone who does not work as a teacher or administrator at the center being evaluated) should complete the PreSET. When the PreSET is being used for research purposes to assess fidelity of PW-PBIS implementation, it is highly recommended that the researchers should be trained in using the PreSET and have a neutral relationship with the early childhood program. For statewide implementation of PBIS, the state's Department of Education should select appropriate personnel to be trained users of the PreSET in their early childhood sites, if at all possible. These users are likely to be different in each state, depending on how resources are allocated and services managed. In Oregon, for example, behavior consultants in each of the seven regions in the state complete PreSETs in the early childhood programs in their areas.

For smaller entities such as nonprofit agencies, child care franchises, and school districts, individuals who already consult with the agency, program, or district should conduct the PreSET. For example, a child care center may have a state-funded prekindergarten classroom in its center and have an inclusion specialist from the state agency who provides onsite professional development to staff members. This inclusion specialist would be an appropriate individual to conduct PreSET administration because this person is a neutral outsider who is already providing consultative services to the center. School districts with public preschool programs may wish to use existing consultants in their systems (e.g., behavior support teachers) as PreSET evaluators. In this way, early childhood systems of service delivery can gain valuable insight from nonemployees while using existing resources to conduct an evaluation of their PW-PBIS implementation.

ORGANIZATION OF THE PreSET MANUAL, FORMS, AND CD-ROM

The PreSET manual provides users with background information about PW-PBIS in early childhood settings and gives directions on administering and scoring the PreSET. The manual was developed to provide guidance and technical assistance to users of the PreSET, as well as center personnel who would like supplemental information for interpreting their PreSET results. The manual provides answers to frequently asked questions about using and scoring the PreSET. A case study is provided for users to practice scoring the PreSET (see Appendix A). All PreSET scoring forms, including the PreSET Administrator Interview Form, PreSET Classroom Interview and Observation Form, PreSET Classroom Summary Form, and the PreSET Scoring Guide are included on the PreSET CD-ROM, sold separately (http://www.brookespublishing.com).

ADMINISTRATION OF THE PreSET

The PreSET should be administered at least once a year, with ideal administration taking place twice a year (once in the fall and once in the spring each academic year). During the initial phases of PW-PBIS implementation (i.e., the first few years), the PreSET should be administered twice a year. Once the center has implemented approximately 80% of PreSET items, the program may choose to reduce PreSET administration to once every fall. The PreSET takes approximately 1 hour to complete in an early childhood program that includes 1–2 classrooms. Administration time is approximately 20 minutes more for each additional classroom in a program.

Implementation of the PreSET first involves an interview with the program administrator using the PreSET Administrator Interview Form and the collection and review of program products (e.g., program handbook, classroom lesson plans, written communication to families). The interview takes approximately 15–20 minutes. Next, observation and interviews are conducted with the lead teacher, other staff, and a sample of children in each classroom of the early childhood program. Information obtained from observations and interviews in each classroom are documented on the PreSET Classroom Interview and Observation Form. One PreSET Classroom Interview and Observation Form should be completed for each classroom in the early childhood program. The evaluator should spend approximately 15–20 minutes in each classroom completing the PreSET Classroom Interview and Observation Form. The PreSET classroom observation includes a specific observation of a transition period from an unstructured or less structured activity (e.g., free play, outdoor play) to a more structured activity (e.g., circle time, snack time) in each classroom. Therefore, knowledge of each classroom's key transitional times will help the evaluator schedule observation times accordingly in each classroom.

After the interview and observation information are collected in each classroom, classroom scores are summarized on the PreSET Classroom Summary Form. Then, scores from the PreSET Classroom Summary Form and PreSET Administrator Interview Form are transferred to the PreSET Scoring Guide to calculate the program's implementation of PW-PBIS by feature for a total PreSET score.

RESEARCH ON THE PreSET

Preliminary evidence indicates that the PreSET is a reliable, valid, and useful tool to measure implementation of universal and program-wide features of PW-PBIS in early childhood classrooms. First, the PreSET is an adaptation of the SET, which has strong psychometric properties (Horner et al., 2001; Vincent et al., 2010). Correlation analyses of SET items indicated an overall α value of .96, which meets or exceeds standard psychometric criteria (Horner et al., 2001). Test–retest reliability and interobserver agreement were strong for the SET, as was its construct validity and sensitivity to change (Horner et al., 2001). An analysis of the SET's psychometric properties indicated that items on the instrument maintained a high internal consistency (Vincent et al., 2010).

Initial analyses have been conducted on the reliability and validity of the PreSET (Steed & Webb, under review). These analyses indicated high internal consistency across the eight PreSET subscales (range .55–.94) and high item-total correlations (range .12–.75). Interrater reliability results were strong, with an average percent agreement of 95% and overall κ value of .80.

Correlations of the PreSET and another validated instrument used to assess implementation of PW-PBIS in early childhood settings, the Teaching Pyramid Observation Tool (TPOT; Fox, Hemmeter, & Snyder, 2008), were used to assess construct validity. Scores from classrooms in which both the PreSET and TPOT were completed were moderately and positively correlated ($r = .33$). Intercorrelations across PreSET subscales were moderate, with a range from .28 to .60, which indicated cohesiveness among the subscales. Finally, PreSET scores from preimplementation and postimplementation data were used to analyze the instrument's sensitivity to change. Paired t test results indicated that mean PreSET scores increased significantly from before to after implementation ($t = 10.49$, $df = 28$, $p < .000$). More information regarding the technical adequacy of the PreSET is provided in Appendix C.

At this time, the PreSET is being used as a primary measure of PW-PBIS implementation in preschools in six states (Nevada, Oregon, New Hampshire, Kentucky, Georgia, and Virginia) and two countries (Canada and South Korea) outside of the United States. It has been used as a measure of PW-PBIS implementation in Head Start classrooms and other early childhood classrooms as part of federally and locally funded grant proposals.

FOR FURTHER INFORMATION

The following list of published research includes the PreSET as a measure or discusses the PreSET's use.

Carter, D.R., & Van Norman, R.K. (2010). Class-wide positive behavior support in preschool: Improving teaching implementation through consultation. *Early Childhood Education Journal, 38,* 279–288.

Carter, D.R., Van Norman, R.K., & Tredwell, C. (2011). Program-wide positive behavior support in preschool: Lessons for getting started. *Early Childhood Education Journal, 38,* 349–355.

Frey, A.J., Boyce, C.A., & Tarullo, L.B. (2009). Implementing positive behavior support in Head Start. In W. Sailor, G. Dunlap, G. Sugai, & H.F. Horner (Eds.), *Handbook of positive behavior support: Special issues in clinical child psychology* (pp. 125–148). New York: Springer.

Frey, A.J., Park, K.L., Browne-Ferrigno, T., & Korfhage, T.L. (2010). The social validity of program-wide positive behavior support. *Journal of Positive Behavior Interventions, 12,* 222–235.

Frey, A., Young, S., Gold, A., & Trevor, E. (2008). Utilizing positive behavior support to achieve integrated mental health services. *National Head Start Association Dialog, 11,* 135–156.

Muscott, H.S., Pomerleau, T., Frey, A., Steed, E.A., Lee, K., & Korfhage, T.L. (in press). *Setting sail for early learning success: Using data-based decision making to measure and monitor outcomes in early childhood programs.*

Muscott, H.S., Pomerleau, T., & Szczesiul, S. (2009). Large-scale implementation of program-wide positive behavioral interventions and supports in early childhood programs in New Hampshire. *NHSA Dialog, 12*(2), 148–169.

Snell, M.E., Stanton-Chapman, T.C., Voorhees, M.D., Berlin, R.A., Hadden, D.S., & McCarty, J.E. (in press). Preschool teachers' reported practices concerning problem behavior and its prevention in Head Start classrooms: Implications for in-service training. *Journal of Positive Behavior Interventions.*

Stanton-Chapman, T.L., Snell, M.E., Doswell, L.C., Voorhees, M.D., McCarty, J.E., & Berlin, R.A. (2011). *Preschool teachers' beliefs about social skills instruction in Head Start classrooms.* Manuscript submitted for publication.

CHAPTER 2

Overview of Program-Wide Positive Behavior Intervention and Support

PURPOSE OF PROGRAM-WIDE POSITIVE BEHAVIOR INTERVENTION AND SUPPORT

Program-wide positive behavior intervention and support (PW-PBIS) has emerged as a model of prevention to increase young children's social-emotional skills and decrease challenging behaviors in early childhood settings (Dunlap & Fox, 2009). PW-PBIS builds upon the foundation of SW-PBIS, which is currently being implemented in schools nationwide. The purpose of SW-PBIS is to switch from a primarily reactive approach to managing challenging behavior to a preventative approach that improves school safety and builds a positive culture in schools (Sugai & Horner, 2002). SW-PBIS includes a focus on using research-based practices that are effective and validated, ensuring that academic and behavioral issues are addressed for all students, and collaborating in a team-based approach to implement change (Sugai & Horner, 2002). SW-PBIS has four essential components (Scott, Alter, Rosenberg, & Borgmeier, 2010):

1. Prediction of when and where challenging behaviors occur
2. Use of effective interventions that prevent challenging behavior, build relationships, provide instruction, and increase student success
3. Consensus among staff to consistently implement agreed-on practices
4. Use of assessments to evaluate the impact of the interventions on key outcomes (e.g., students' behavior)

Approximately 20% of young children in the general population and 70% of young children with special needs engage in significant challenging behavior (Strain, Joseph, & Hemmeter, 2009). Child care providers have reported that more young children are engaging in more severe challenging behaviors at a younger age (Joseph & Strain, 2008). With an increase in the number of young children displaying challenging behavior in early learning environments, it is clear that a model like PW-PBIS should be applied to these educational contexts as well.

SW-PBIS, the model proposed for older school children and school systems, requires adaptation for young children and early childhood systems of service delivery for several reasons. First, early childhood systems of service delivery (e.g., early intervention, Head Start, publicly funded prekindergarten, private child care) are more diverse and fragmented than the public school system for K–12 education in the United States (Fox & Hemmeter, 2009). Early childhood programs are less likely to contain resources, such as planning time and access to mental health consultants, than K–12 public education settings. Furthermore, early childhood educators and administrators are less likely to be well trained on evidence-based practices to support young children's social-emotional development or data collection systems to document challenging behavior (Fox & Hemmeter, 2009). Finally, young children have different developmental needs than students in elementary, middle, and high school. Therefore, the interventions and strategies that are key components of SW-PBIS need to be adapted for use in early childhood environments.

Initial proposals for adaptations of the SW-PBIS model for early childhood included such things as ensuring that universal level rules and expectations were written in developmentally appropriate language that young children could understand (Benedict, Horner, & Squires, 2007). Other suggestions included a focus on family involvement because family collaboration is a key element of early childhood education (Fox & Hemmeter, 2009), as well as providing professional development to early childhood educators in data collection and behavior management strategies because preschool teachers are less likely to have received this training in their high school or college-level coursework (Stormont, Lewis, & Beckner, 2005).

In 2003, a new framework for implementing PW-PBIS in early childhood settings was developed and proposed. The Teaching Pyramid (Fox, Dunlap, Hemmeter, Joseph, & Strain, 2003) defined the continuum of supports that would build positive relationships between teachers and children and prevent young children's challenging behavior (Hemmeter, Ostrosky, & Fox, 2006). The Teaching Pyramid is a framework built on supportive and positive relationships between children, families, and professionals, with four levels of support to address the needs of all children (Fox et al., 2003). It was modeled after tiered prevention and intervention frameworks in public health (Fox & Hemmeter, 2009). Faculty at the federally funded TACSEI and CSEFEL centers developed the Teaching Pyramid and modified it into the Pyramid Model for Supporting Social-Emotional Development in Infants and Young Children (see Figure 2.1; http://csefel.vanderbilt.edu/); they have since documented its usefulness as a sound framework for early childhood settings (TACSEI, 2011). The purpose of PW-PBIS is to address the behavioral and social needs of children in educational contexts. The Teaching Pyramid provides specific, research-based, and developmentally appropriate practices that can be implemented in early childhood settings to meet this goal (Dunlap & Fox, 2009).

Research investigating the impact of PW-PBIS in early childhood settings and application of the Teaching Pyramid initially focused on individualized supports for children with the most challenging behavior. In these studies, teachers were taught to implement behavior support plans or other specific prevention or consequence strategies to reduce preschoolers' challenging behavior (e.g., Blair, Fox, & Lentini, 2010; Duda, Dunlap, Fox, Lentini, & Clarke, 2004). This research has demonstrated that early childhood teachers can effectively use strategies associated with the tertiary level of PW-PBIS in their classrooms to ameliorate individual children's challenging behavior. Other research has shown that teachers can be taught to use universal PW-PBIS strategies that focus on building relationships, establishing clear expectations, and preventing the challenging behavior of all children in a preschool classroom (Benedict et al., 2007; Carter & Van Norman, 2010).

Universal PW-PBIS strategies taught to preschool teachers include such things as developing and using a visual schedule to mark the order of classroom routines, developing and teaching classroom rules, and using precorrection prior to misbehavior. Benedict, Horner, and Squires, (2007) taught four early childhood teachers to use these universal PW-PBIS strategies in their classrooms; these teachers found the use of universal PW-PBIS strategies in their classroom to be valuable and appropriate for young children. Carter and Van Norman (2010) replicated these findings regarding teachers' abilities to implement strategies at the universal level of PW-PBIS in their classrooms. The researchers extended the literature base by demonstrating that teachers' use of universal PW-PBIS strategies had a positive impact on children's academic engagement (Carter & Van Norman, 2010). Another study documented that early childhood educators viewed PW-PBIS positively and felt that its basic tenets and purpose are important for their work with young children (Frey, Park, Browne-Ferrigno & Korfage, 2010).

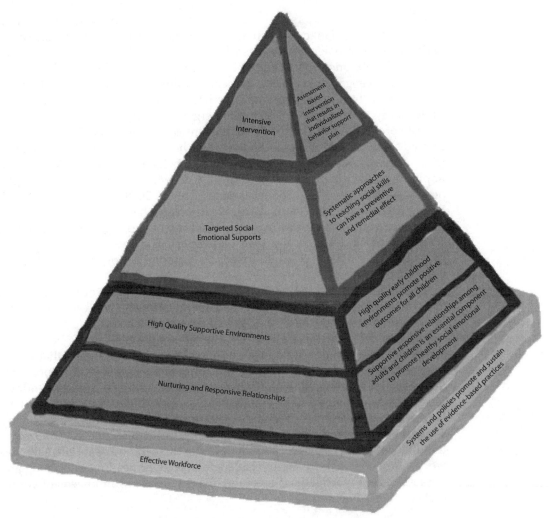

Figure 2.1.   Pyramid model for supporting social-emotional competence in infants and young children. (From http://csefel.vanderbilt. edu/; reprinted by permission.)

CHILDREN WITH CHALLENGING BEHAVIOR

One of the primary missions of PW-PBIS is to reduce and prevent challenging behavior in very young children (Dunlap & Fox, 2009). Many young children demonstrate challenging behavior, such as hitting, biting, and having tantrums during their early development. Although challenging behavior is a typical component of early childhood development, an increasing number of very young children demonstrate a high rate or intensity of behavior problems (Strain et al., 2009). Research on the prevalence of behavior problems in young children conducted in the 1980s indicated that approximately 10%–15% of preschoolers exhibited mild to moderate behavior problems (e.g., Cornely & Bromet, 1986). Researchers now estimate that approximately 20% of the general population of young children exhibit significant challenging behavior and that 25% of preschoolers meet the criteria for oppositional defiant disorder (Strain et al., 2009; Webster-Stratton, 2000). Approximately 22%–39% of preschoolers with risk factors such as poverty exhibit clinically significant levels of problem behaviors (Kaiser, Cai, Hancock, & Foster, 2002) and approximately 70% of children with identified special needs exhibit challenging behaviors (Strain et al., 2009).

Challenging behaviors that are exhibited during the preschool years may persist and develop into more dangerous patterns of behavior in later childhood and even adulthood. Early behavior problems have been linked with conduct disorders in adolescence and adulthood, substance abuse, and delinquency (Patterson, Reid, & Dishion, 1992). Young children who engage in challenging behavior are also at increased risk of being expelled and excluded from child care and preschool classrooms. A study conducted at the Yale Child Study Center found that prekindergarten students were expelled at three times the rate of children in Grades K–12 (Gilliam & Shabar, 2006). The rate of expulsion decreased significantly if the preschool teachers had access to a behavioral consultant to help them manage young children's challenging behavior. This provides important policy implications for the provision of help for teachers in the form of on-the-ground mental health consultation (Frey, Young, Gold, & Trevor, 2008; Gilliam & Shabar, 2006; Green, Everhart, Gordon, & Gettman, 2006). Preschool teachers may not have the training and/or the capacity with their staffing ratios to effectively manage the number of children with social-emotional difficulties in their classrooms. They need access to professionals who can support their use of research-based interventions to address children's emotional and behavioral challenges.

Many successful and effective approaches that reduce young children's challenging behaviors have been developed. These interventions involve completing a functional behavioral assessment (FBA) for a child to determine the function (e.g., escape or avoidance; access to preferred activities, people, or objects) of the challenging behavior. A behavioral support plan is then developed that indicates the teacher strategies that should be used to prevent challenging behavior, teach replacement behaviors, and respond to any continued challenging behavior. Research has indicated that the FBA process and function-based interventions are effective for young children with challenging behavior (Wood, Blair, & Ferro, 2010). However, early childhood professionals do not always develop behavioral support plans that include all required components and use the key informants who know the child best, such as the child's parents or teachers (Wood et al., 2010). Professionals who work with young children with challenging behavior need more training and support to implement best practices and meet the diverse mental health needs of young children in early care environments.

KEY FEATURES OF PW-PBIS

One approach to designing interventions that will produce sustainable reductions in problem behavior includes the use of a continuum of behavioral supports known as PBIS. This three-tiered approach to intervention uses a system perspective that is based on the principles of behavior analysis, inclusion, and person-centered planning (Carr et al., 2002; Horner & Sugai, 2000; Koegel, Koegel, & Dunlap, 1996). The PBIS model includes practical strategies for intervening to reduce problem behaviors and includes a team-based approach to assessment, intervention, and administrative support (Sugai & Horner, 2002). The focus on socially meaningful strategies and the collaborative nature of PBIS has increased its acceptance and effectiveness in educational and human service settings (Sugai & Horner, 2002).

The PW-PBIS model was adapted from the larger PBIS framework for use with young children. It includes tiered support to address the differential needs of all children, small groups of children who require a little more support, and individual children who have more intensive needs (Dunlap & Fox, 2009). The PW-PBIS model maintains the primary focus of the PBIS framework on prevention, data-based decision making, and systemwide change. There are three levels of preventative intervention and support in the PW-PBIS model, as well as the use of leadership teams, data collection strategies for evaluation and decision-making processes, and the provision of adequate resources (e.g., materials, training, time) to support sustained implementation (Dunlap & Fox, 2009).

The three levels of support in a PW-PBIS model are the

1. *Primary level:* Universal prevention, which includes establishing nurturing and responsive relationships and providing high-quality supportive learning environments
2. *Secondary level:* Targeted prevention, which includes the direct instruction of social-emotional skills to small groups of children who do not respond to universal supports
3. *Tertiary level:* Intensive individualized interventions for children who do not respond to universal or social skill interventions or who engage in high-intensity or chronic challenging behaviors

These levels of PW-PBIS are defined further in the Pyramid Model, a framework that provides specific descriptions of PW-PBIS strategies and supports that should be used in early childhood environments (see Figure 2.1). Each level of support is described further in the following sections.

Primary Level: Universal Prevention

At the primary level of prevention, all children are provided with a safe, organized, and predictable environment with a focus on building positive relationships between children, families, and program staff. Attention is given to the design of each classroom (e.g., well-defined learning centers), adherence to a schedule that flows naturally from structured (e.g., circle time) to unstructured (e.g., free play) activities, and frequent positive interactions with children and families.

Defining Expectations

One important aspect of creating a positive learning environment and social culture in an early childhood center is to communicate the social behaviors that are expected. These expectations or rules should be decided at the program level using input from teachers, children, and families. The expectations should then be adopted in every classroom. Programs should decide upon three to five of the most important expectations. Each expectation should be developmentally appropriate and use simple and positive language.

The expectations should be visually represented for children in the form of a poster. The poster should use pictures and words of each expectation and be displayed at the children's eye level in at least one location in each classroom. The poster should include the written rules, as well as accompanying pictures of children engaging in the rules or easily interpretable symbols of the rules. An example of a classroom rules poster is provided in Figure 2.2.

Matrix of Classroom Rules

Because of the general nature of program-wide expectations or rules, it is advisable for classrooms to identify behavioral expectations that align with each classroom routine. Each classroom rule should be defined by clear, positively stated behaviors that are expected of children during each classroom routine. Figure 2.3 provides an example of a matrix of classroom rules based on the program rules *take care of ourselves, take care of each other*, and *take care of our things*.

Teaching Behavioral Expectations

The program expectations or rules must be taught to children in each classroom. Explicit teaching of program expectations should occur frequently (e.g., every day in the beginning

Figure 2.2.   Classroom rules poster. (Photo taken by Lisa Wells; poster developed by Lisa Wells.)

of the year). Large-group activities, such as circle time, are logical and appropriate activities in which to teach and review the expectations. Children may also benefit from explicit instruction of program rules in small groups. Effective teaching practices include providing children with opportunities to see, hear, and practice the skills, as well as opportunities to be recognized for demonstrating appropriate behaviors. Children should be able to see the expectations in pictures on rules posters, hear the rules spoken in positively stated language, and practice the rules by role play or "pretending" activities. Children should also be positively acknowledged for demonstrating the rules appropriately.

Daily routines	Take care of ourselves	Take care of each other	Take care of our things
Arrival	• Walk to our cubbies • Join play nicely	• Say hello to others	• Put things away
Free play and outside	• Follow directions • Ask for help (if we need it)	• Join play nicely • Include others • Share • Take turns • Use our words	• Treat things safely • Put things away
Circle	• Sit on mat • Participate	• Take turns • Follow directions • Keep hands and feet in spot	• Clear away mats • Hang up jobs
Snack	• Follow directions • Face the table • Keep hands and feet in spot	• Use our manners • Answer others	• Put things away

Figure 2.3.   Matrix of classroom rules: Teaching behavioral expectations.

Sample Song for Teaching Expectations
(Sung to the tune of "The Farmer in the Dell")

We follow classroom rules	We always make safe choices
We follow classroom rules	We always make safe choices
Every day, here at school	Every day, at work and play
We follow classroom rules	We always make safe choices
We are kind to our friends	We take care of our things
We are kind to our friends	We take care of our things
Every day, at work and play	Every day, at work and play
We are kind to our friends	We take care of our things

Figure 2.4. Sample song.

When explicitly teaching classroom rules, teachers should review the rules poster, pointing to each rule and the accompanying picture(s) while stating the rule. Children should be encouraged to repeat the classroom rules. It is common in early childhood settings to incorporate fun approaches to teaching children the program rules, such as creating a song using a popular tune, creating a fingerplay for the program rules, or incorporating the use of a mascot to teach the rules (e.g., using a bumblebee puppet to teach the "Big B" rules). An example song written to the tune of "The Farmer in the Dell" is included in Figure 2.4.

The teacher may then model examples and nonexamples of rule-following behaviors. Young children often find it very funny when teachers model nonexamples of rule-following behavior. Teachers should be sure to minimize the exaggeration of nonexamples so as not to make the inappropriate example more appealing than the appropriate example, however. Children should then have the opportunity to practice following the rules, with children volunteering to demonstrate the behaviors that go with each rule. Expected behaviors should be taught and practiced during the routine or in the location in which they would naturally occur (e.g., using Figure 2.3, teach and practice *use our manners* in the context of snack time and *include others* in the context of outside play).

Teachers should have a plan for explicitly teaching and acknowledging the agreed-on rules in their classrooms. One way to accomplish this is to develop and implement lesson plans or "cool tools" that describe the purpose of the lesson, including teacher behaviors, child behaviors, and follow-up activities that will be involved in the lesson. An example of a "cool tool" or Classroom Rules Lesson Plan, is provided in Figure 2.5.

It is important that children have practice seeing the rules, hearing the rules, saying the rules, and practicing the rules throughout the day. One way to accomplish this is to provide visual reminders of the classroom rules in multiple locations in the classroom.

Responding to Children's Appropriate and Challenging Behavior

Children should receive acknowledgment when they follow classroom rules and engage in other appropriate social behaviors throughout the day. How children will be acknowledged for following expectations should be decided at the program level for consistency across classrooms. The system of acknowledgement should be age appropriate, limit distractions in the classroom (i.e., be brief), limit competition between students, and maximize teacher flexibility so that an individual teacher could modify the system based on the student characteristics of his or her classroom.

In a program-wide acknowledgement system, teachers provide children with discrete feedback (e.g., providing a child with a cotton ball to put in a jar, giving the child a "caring" leaf to put on a tree poster) immediately following desired prosocial or rule following behaviors (e.g., after the child shares a toy with another child). Children should collectively work toward a class goal to earn a special event such as a pajama party, silly hat day, or bubble-blowing party after they have reached their target (e.g., filling the jar with cotton

---

Classroom Rules Lesson Plan

Rule: We Care for Others   Teachers: Ms. Jackson and Mr. King

Introduction of the rule:

1. Read *Bear Feels Sick* by Karma Wilson (with Jane Chapman; Margaret K. McElderry, 2007) to the children.
2. Ask children questions throughout the book, focusing on the word *care* and what it means to care for others. Example questions:

   "What do you think it means to care for others?"

   "What is something someone can do to show they care?"

   "How did the animals care for the bear?"
3. After reading the story, ask children to demonstrate the rule. Use the answers that the children generated in response to the questions:

   If a child answered that you can show you care by helping someone, have a child show the class what helping looks like.

   If a child answered that caring means hugging, have a child show the class a hug.

Teaching example:

1. Show the children cards that were created for each part of the teaching matrix with a picture of a child in the classroom caring for others.
2. Show them the poster board with the headings Circle, Free Play, Outside, and Snack that have pictures to go with the words of each routine.
3. Model putting one picture of caring for others (e.g., passing fruit to a friend) under a routine heading (e.g., snack). Talk through why you put this picture under "snack."
4. Have the children take turns placing a picture of caring for others under a heading on the board. Ask each child why he or she put it there and ask the others if they agree or disagree. Keep in mind that there are no real "right" and "wrong" answers for this.

Class discussion:

1. Ask the children questions to facilitate discussion about why we follow the rule to care for others. Example questions:

   Why do we need to care for others?

   What might happen if no one cares for anyone?

   How do other people feel when we care about them?

   What do you think might happen to you if you care for someone else?

Follow-up activities:

1. During the final circle time of the day, ask the children what they did that day to care for others during circle, free play, outside, and snack.
2. Notice and verbally praise children when they exhibit caring behaviors across routines.
3. Leave another set of picture cards of the children following the rule in the writing center; let them use the pictures to write stories or draw pictures about caring for others in their journals.
4. Provide a medicine kit and other materials (e.g., prescription pad and pens) in the housekeeping area for children to recreate some of the caring behaviors from the *Bear Feels Sick* book.

Figure 2.5.   Example of a "cool tool" Classroom Rules Lesson Plan.

balls, filling the tree poster with leaves). Programs should decide on the acknowledgment system that they will use across all classrooms. The acknowledgment system should be feasible for teachers to implement, pay attention to resources and cost (e.g., a pizza party is much more costly than a bubble-blowing party), and provide opportunities for children to give input (e.g., asking the children what they want to work toward). In the following example, an early childhood program uses an acknowledgment system in each classroom in which teachers provide children with a cotton ball after instances in which children exhibit targeted cooperation behaviors.

Cooperation should be defined with children as any positive collaboration with another peer or adult. It includes such things as working with another peer to complete a puzzle, digging holes while another child plants seeds in the garden, or following a teacher's directions to put on a coat before going outside to play. Each time that an adult recognizes that a child has cooperated with a peer or another teacher, the teacher can give the child a cotton ball and use specific verbal praise (e.g., "I liked how you and Natasha cooperated to pick up the carpet squares together"). The children can put the cotton balls in the cooperation jar; when the jar is full, the class gets to have a dance party during their next morning circle time. During this circle time, the teacher should discuss how well the children cooperated with others, show them the full jar, and remind them of the choices they have during the dance party to dress up, move their bodies safely, and sit down when the music ends. The teacher can provide options for the children to dress up (e.g., boas, hats, large shoes), allow children to select the songs they dance to, and allow them to dance for about 6 minutes before settling into the rest of circle time. The teacher and children then should empty the cooperation jar and start over with a new target goal and special event. An image of the cooperation jar used in this program is provided in Figure 2.6 as an example of a program-wide acknowledgment system.

Figure 2.6.   Example of a cooperation jar. (Photo taken by Cori Wixson; jar idea developed by Samantha Mann.)

Children can be encouraged to use appropriate social behaviors in other ways as well. Teachers can use a high ratio of positive comments (e.g., praise, approval) to negative comments (e.g., reprimand, correction, disapproval) when speaking to children in their classrooms, use specific verbal praise after a child engages in an appropriate behavior (e.g., "Thanks for sharing your toy with Shaheen. You were being a good friend!"), and use precorrection to remind a child of an expectation or rule before a situation occurs (e.g., "Remember to use your walking feet when you line up to go outside," "Please use your quiet voices when we go back to the classroom").

In addition to establishing program-wide methods of acknowledging appropriate social behaviors, each program should also decide how adults will respond to children's challenging behavior. A behavior incident flowchart can be helpful for staff in a program to know how to respond appropriately after a child exhibits challenging behavior. It is important that the behavior incident flowchart includes a description of which behaviors are to be addressed, definitions (or a reference to definitions) of the reportable challenging behaviors, and the individuals within the program who should be involved in any reporting procedures. Figure 2.7 provides an example of a behavior incident flow chart that the New Hampton Child Care Center in New Hampshire developed and follows when responding to young children's challenging behavior.

The establishment of a programmatic response procedure for addressing challenging behavior is an essential component of PW-PBIS. Documentation procedures should include the collection of data on challenging behaviors, a data entry program that will summarize the data, and a system for the program leadership team to regularly review and analyze the information for data-based decision-making processes. Data may be used to begin a targeted intervention with a small group of children, initiate more intensive intervention with individual children, or make changes to individual children's behavioral support plans. These data may also be used to make programmatic or individualized changes to the PW-PBIS system (e.g., increased teacher planning time, additional professional development opportunities) based on the information collected.

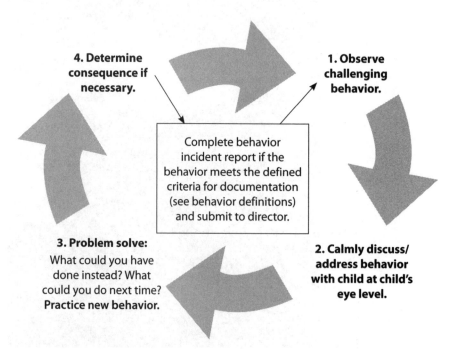

4. Determine consequence if necessary.

1. Observe challenging behavior.

Complete behavior incident report if the behavior meets the defined criteria for documentation (see behavior definitions) and submit to director.

3. Problem solve: What could you have done instead? What could you do next time? **Practice new behavior.**

2. Calmly discuss/ address behavior with child at child's eye level.

Figure 2.7.   Behavior incident flow chart. (From New Hampton Child Care Center; reprinted by permission.)

The Behavior Incident Reporting System–New Hampshire (BIRS-NH) is a web-based data management system created specifically to help early childhood programs use behavior incident data to design program-wide, classroom, and individualized positive behavioral intervention and supports. BIRS-NH is a software system for collecting, aggregating, and summarizing incidents of challenging behavior within the contexts that they occur. Summary data are easily presented in visual form for review and analysis. BIRS-NH includes the necessary components for a programmatic response system in early childhood settings, including the categories and definitions for documenting 10 challenging behaviors specific to early childhood, the routines in which they occur, and staff/administrative responses.

Teacher/staff responses noted on the BIRS-NH system include such possibilities as reteaching the social skill, providing a verbal reminder of a classroom rule, providing physical guidance, or making a curricular modification. These potential teacher responses should be based on the child's behavioral support plan, if such a plan has been developed. For example, if 5-year-old Takumi's behavioral support plan indicates that he should be reminded to use his words and prompted to verbally choose an alternative activity at the start of a tantrum, his teachers should use these responses during the tantrum and then choose these options in the BIRS-NH system when documenting the behavior incident.

In the absence of an FBA and behavioral support plan, teachers should respond to a child's challenging behavior based on the perceived function, severity, and context of the behavior. For example, if 4-year-old Veronica hits another child while playing in the sandbox, the teachers may remind Veronica of the program-wide rule to care for others and provide subsequent individualized teaching of appropriate play (e.g., sharing toys, asking for a toy from a friend). These responses would be used to manage the immediate situation and teach replacement behaviors for Veronica's hitting behavior. The responses and the context of the behavior incident would be documented in the BIRS-NH System.

Teacher/staff responses should not inadvertently reinforce the challenging behavior, be too severe for the child's behavior, or neglect to take into consideration the influence of environmental variables (e.g., transition, other children, change in schedule). For example, if Benny screams during circle time and an FBA has indicated that his screaming behavior functions to escape from circle, especially when he is not involved in circle activities (i.e., he is bored), it would not be appropriate to remove Benny from circle when he screams. Removing him from the circle would likely reinforce the screaming behavior and make it more likely that Benny would scream in the future during circle time. An alternative response, such as expelling Benny from school for the day, would be inappropriate as well because this response is too severe for the child's behavior. Instead, a modification should be used in this situation to prevent Benny from screaming, such as having Benny help during circle time (e.g., by setting up the chairs), giving all of the children manipulatives (e.g., felt pieces) to use during book reading, and/or sitting close to a teacher during circle time.

Some teacher responses indicated on the BIRS-NH form (e.g., removal from activity) are not appropriate for some children and challenging behaviors or may not be approved for use in some settings. For example, some early childhood agencies no longer allow teachers to use removal as a response to children's challenging behavior, and timeout has never been a proposed behavior management strategy within the PW-PBIS framework. However, because some early childhood teachers do use removal from area or activity as a response to challenging behavior, it appears in the array of options in the BIRS-NH system. Early childhood programs may eliminate such responses from their data collection forms as necessary and appropriate.

An example behavioral incident report, based on the categories included in the BIRS-NH data management system, is provided in Figure 2.8. Examples of behavior

NH CEBIS
New Hampshire Center for Effective
Behavioral Interventions and Supports

Behavior Incident Report

Child's name/code: _____ Program: _____ Classroom: _____

Date: _____ Time of occurrence: _____ Referring staff: _____

Severity: Mild   Moderate   Severe

ROUTINE (check one)

- ❏ Arrival
- ❏ Classroom jobs
- ❏ Circle/large group activity
- ❏ Small group activity
- ❏ Centers/workshops

- ❏ Meals
- ❏ Quiet time/nap
- ❏ Outdoor play
- ❏ Special activity/field trip
- ❏ Self-care/bathroom
- ❏ Transition

- ❏ Departure
- ❏ Clean-up
- ❏ Therapy
- ❏ Individual activity
- ❏ Free play
- ❏ Other _____

MOTIVATION (check up to 2)

- ❏ Obtain desired item
- ❏ Obtain desired activity
- ❏ Gain peer attention

- ❏ Gain adult attention
- ❏ Obtain sensory
- ❏ Avoid task/activity
- ❏ Avoid peers

- ❏ Avoid adults
- ❏ Avoid sensory
- ❏ Don't know
- ❏ Other _____

CHALLENGING BEHAVIOR (check up to 3)

- ❏ Physical aggression
- ❏ Self injury
- ❏ Disruption/Tantrum
- ❏ Inappropriate language

- ❏ Verbal aggression
- ❏ Noncompliance
- ❏ Social withdrawal/isolation

- ❏ Running away
- ❏ Property damage
- ❏ Unsafe behaviors
- ❏ Other _____

INVOLVED PERSONS (check all that apply)

- ❏ Assistant teacher
- ❏ Peers
- ❏ Other _____

- ❏ Teacher
- ❏ None
- ❏ Substitute

- ❏ Support/admin. staff
- ❏ Family member
- ❏ Therapist

TEACHER/STAFF RESPONSE (check the most intrusive)

- ❏ Re-Teach/practice
- ❏ Verbal reminder
- ❏ Remove from area
- ❏ Physical guidance

- ❏ Curriculum modification
- ❏ Family contact
- ❏ Loss of item/privilege
- ❏ Move within group

- ❏ Time with adult in different classroom/support staff
- ❏ Remove from activity
- ❏ Physical hold/Restrain
- ❏ Other _____

ADMINISTRATIVE FOLLOW-UP (check the most intrusive)

- ❏ Nonapplicable
- ❏ Talk with child
- ❏ Telephone contact with parent/family

- ❏ Parent/family meeting
- ❏ Reduce hours in program
- ❏ Arrange behavioral consultation/team

- ❏ Targeted group intervention
- ❏ Transfer to another program
- ❏ Dismissal
- ❏ Other _____

Comments: _____

_____

_____

Revised 12/09

Figure 2.8. Behavior incident report. (From New Hampshire Center for Effective Behavioral Interventions and Supports [2009]. *BIRS-NH Data Collection Form.* Bedford, NH: New Hampshire Center for Effective Behavioral Interventions and Supports; reprinted by permission.)

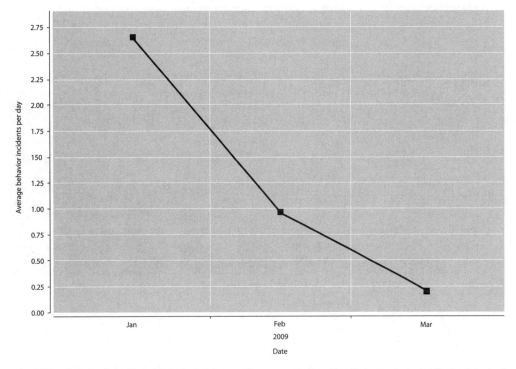

Figure 2.9. Behavior chart: Average behavior incidents per day per month. (From New Hampshire Center for Effective Behavioral Interventions and Supports [2009]. *Behavior Incident Reporting System-NH*. Bedford, NH: New Hampshire Center for Effective Behavioral Interventions and Supports; reprinted by permission.)

charts that are generated from this data management system are also included (see Figures 2.9–2.11).

The BIRS-NH system was developed by Howard Muscott and Tina Pomerleau of the New Hampshire Center for Effective Behavioral Interventions and Supports [NH CEBIS] at the Southeastern Regional Education Service Center [SERESC], in collaboration with Lise Fox from the Louis De La Parte Florida Mental Health Institute at the University of South Florida, along with the valued input of public and private preschool and Head Start programs. The authors would like to acknowledge Charles F. Munat, Software Developer, of Lightsource Web Works [LightsourceWebWorks.com] for the development of the BIRS-NH software.

Organized and Predictable Environment

Children are more likely to exhibit appropriate classroom behaviors when they know what activities to expect throughout the day. One way to accomplish this is to have a classroom schedule that includes words and visuals of the day's activities, which is posted at children's eye level. Teachers should point to the pictures and verbally discuss the day's activities during a large-group meeting and/or throughout the day with small groups or individual children who may need reminders about what to expect from the next routine. It may be helpful to use a visual prompt (e.g., an arrow) that can be moved down the schedule as the day progresses to indicate the current routine. Figure 2.12 shows a classroom schedule in which the teacher and children move a monkey image down the schedule prior to making the transition to each routine.

Another key component of a classroom's predictability is the manner in which transitions occur between activities. Children are more likely to make the transition to a new activity while following classroom expectations if they are warned of the transition in advance. This is especially important for transitions from a less structured activity (e.g.,

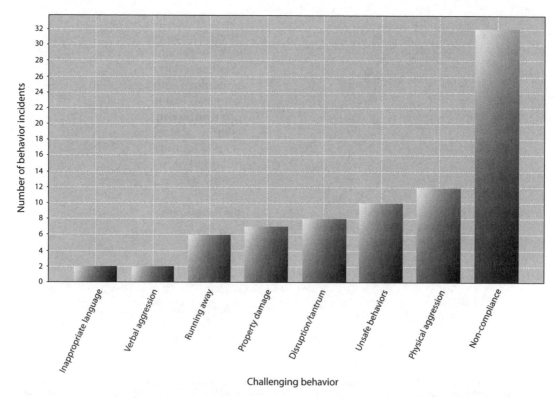

Figure 2.10.   Behavior chart: Behavior incidents by challenging behavior. (From New Hampshire Center for Effective Behavioral Interventions and Supports [2009]. *Behavior Incident Reporting System-NH*. Bedford, NH: New Hampshire Center for Effective Behavioral Interventions and Supports; reprinted by permission.)

free play, outside play) to a more structured activity (e.g., circle time, math). Verbal warnings usually include references to the amount of time left prior to the transition (e.g., "2 more minutes of play"). Once it is time for the transition to occur, it is also helpful to provide a signal other than (or in addition to) a verbal direction. Examples of common and easy-to-use transition signals include turning the lights off and on, playing or singing a song, or ringing a bell.

Family Involvement

Commensurate with all early childhood efforts, PW-PBIS efforts should actively involve families. Families should be notified of a program's practices to support children's social-emotional development, including program rules, how challenging behavior will be managed in the classroom, when families will be notified of behavioral incidents, and how families can participate in and support PW-PBIS in the program and at home. This communication may be done verbally (e.g., at a welcome night, through regular communication with families), but should also occur in writing (e.g., program handbook, newsletter).

In addition to communicating general PW-PBIS practices, program administrators and classroom teachers should communicate with families regularly about how children are doing in their social-emotional development. This communication may occur naturally at pickup or drop-off times, but should also include phone calls, e-mail communication, regularly scheduled parent–teacher conferences, and/or letters that are regularly sent home to families. Families should also be encouraged to participate in program activities. Families may be invited to be involved as classroom visitors to read a book or play music during

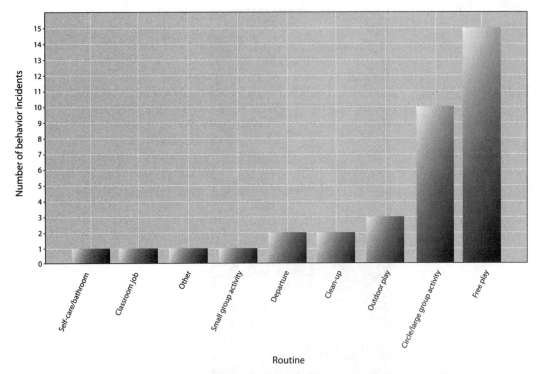

Figure 2.11. Behavior chart: Behavior incidents by routine. (From New Hampshire Center for Effective Behavioral Interventions and Supports [2009]. *Behavior Incident Reporting System-NH.* Bedford, NH: New Hampshire Center for Effective Behavioral Interventions and Supports; reprinted by permission.)

circle time, chaperone children on field trips, help teachers plan and put on a special event, or participate by providing needed classroom items and materials for specific projects.

Secondary Social-Emotional Interventions

The secondary level of support involves targeted interventions for children who require additional assistance with their social skills. In SW-PBIS, secondary interventions usually involve a specific targeted intervention such as Check-in/Check-out (Filter et al., 2007; Scott et al., 2010). Check-in/Check-out involves a student checking in with an adult at the beginning of the school day to receive a point card with the school rules, as well as boxes for each class period in which a teacher rates the student on a 1–4 scale after each class period. At the end of the school day, the student takes his or her completed card to the designated adult to check out, which involves counting his or her points and receiving reinforcement (e.g., selecting an item from a bin or special privilege) if an adequate number of points were achieved that day (Filter et al., 2007). These targeted interventions are provided to a small group of children who do not respond to universal prevention strategies but who do not exhibit such severe challenging behavior that they require individualized support. Targeted interventions are designed to be efficient interventions that may be applied in the same way to a group of students who may benefit from an increase in positive adult attention throughout the school day (Filter et al., 2007). In this way, significant resources are not used to address students' needs at the second level of SW-PBIS.

Secondary interventions have not been clearly identified in the PW-PBIS model for early childhood classrooms. There have been some proposals to modify the Check-in/Check-out procedure for early childhood (Hawken & Johnston, 2007; Steed, 2011).

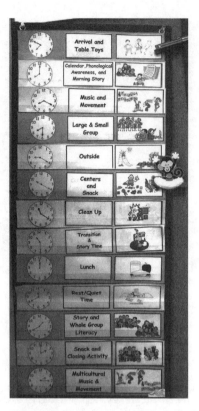

Figure 2.12. Classroom schedule. (Photo taken by Cori Wixson; schedule developed by Samantha Mann.)

However, no one has systematically implemented or researched a secondary intervention such as the Check-in/Check-out procedure with preschoolers. Secondary interventions for preschoolers may include teacher-implemented strategies that are used throughout the day (e.g., working with several children who are learning to wait for one's turn). However, limited prepared resources (e.g., lesson plans, scripts) are currently available for early childhood teachers to teach social skills, emotional literacy, emotional awareness, social problem solving, sharing, or coming up with play ideas to children who need this support.

Various social skills programs are evidence based and commercially available (e.g., Powell & Dunlap, 2009). However, most programs are expensive, often require professional development to implement, and are usually provided to a whole classroom of children, which eliminates the efficiency and effectiveness of a targeted intervention for just those children who need the extra support. Young children who require the secondary level of support are likely to require small-group instruction to learn new skills and generalize them to new contexts (e.g., play).

The PreSET does not specifically evaluate a preschool program's use of secondary, targeted social-emotional supports. Preschools interested in investing in their secondary level of interventions are encouraged to use other resources, such as the review of evidence-based social skills curricula by Powell and Dunlap (2009) or the training materials developed by the CSEFEL (http://csefel.vanderbilt.edu).

Tertiary Intensive Individualized Interventions

Individualized interventions are provided to children in the classroom who do not respond to other prevention efforts and who exhibit chronic and/or severe challenging behavior.

Individualized interventions should be based on the function of the child's behavior and be practical. Interventions should consider teachers' training, available time, and resources for implementing and evaluating the intervention.

A preschool program may not have any children who require an individualized intervention. However, every preschool program should have a system in place, such as social-emotional screening procedures to identify children who would require such an intervention. Social-emotional screening procedures involve completing social-emotional screening instruments such as the Ages & Stages Questionnaires®: Social-Emotional (Squires, Bricker, & Twombly, 2002) when teachers, parents, or other individuals who interact with a child have concerns about the child's challenging behavior or social-emotional development. It is often most useful to have multiple informants (e.g., the child's teacher and primary caregiver) complete a social-emotional screening assessment to compare the results across contexts and provide a more complete picture of the routines and environments in which the child is having difficulties.

In addition to being familiar with screening procedures, preschool teachers should also know the process for requesting a behavioral referral. For example, in some preschool classrooms, when a child engages in severe challenging behavior (e.g., chronic hitting of others), a preschool teacher may request a behavioral referral and receive support from a behavior or mental health consultant to complete an FBA and develop a behavioral intervention plan. An FBA and behavioral intervention plan are always implemented as part of a program's tertiary interventions for children who exhibit severe and/or chronic challenging behavior.

The PreSET does not specifically evaluate a preschool program's use of tertiary individualized interventions. Preschools interested in learning more about the FBA process and how to develop behavioral intervention plans are encouraged to use other resources, such as the training materials developed by the CSEFEL (http://csefel.vanderbilt.edu) and/or to use the expertise of mental health and behavior consultants in their area.

USING PW-PBIS

PW-PBIS is built on a foundation of systemwide resources and policies, such as a well-trained workforce, administrative support, and access to information and resources that promote and sustain the use of evidence-based practices. These systemic features must include a leadership team to guide implementation of PW-PBIS within the preschool or program; data collection procedures to evaluate classroom and child outcomes; and sufficient funding, resources, and professional development for administrators and teachers to implement PW-PBIS.

The purpose of the PW-PBIS leadership team is to bring together multiple perspectives on instituting programmatic and systemic changes across the program that will address challenging behaviors and increase social-emotional skills. The leadership team should meet approximately once a month and organize its meeting around goals and objectives outlined in the team's action plan, including aspects of PW-PBIS implementation that are in progress or not yet implemented.

In a preschool classroom, the PW-PBIS leadership team may include lead and assistant classroom teachers, administrators, bus drivers, kitchen staff, classroom volunteers, family representatives, and related services personnel (e.g., mental health specialists, speech-language pathologists). Essentially, the PW-PBIS leadership team should include all adults who regularly interact with children in the preschool program, whether that interaction takes place in the classroom, gymnasium, playground, or bus. The program should include families in the PW-PBIS leadership team. However, families should not be included if the PW-PBIS leadership team is likely to discuss individual children's challenging behavior or prevention/intervention strategies used for individual children, as it will breach confidentiality.

Data should be collected on classroom and program features of PW-PBIS so that PW-PBIS efforts may be evaluated on an ongoing basis. Although the practice of collecting data in an early childhood setting is challenging, it is possible to develop and implement feasible data collection systems that provide important information for teachers and administrators. First, when evaluating the implementation of features of PW-PBIS, data should be collected with a tool designed for this purpose, such as the PreSET. Other program-wide data collection procedures should be used, including observation forms to track important teacher practices (e.g., number of positive statements made to children) and student behaviors (e.g., prosocial and challenging behaviors). It may also be important to track such things as teacher and child injuries, behavioral referrals for consultation, the amount of time a behavioral consultant spends in the classroom, and the number of telephone calls and/or meetings with families.

Data on system-level features may also be important to assess, including the time allowed for teachers' preparation, the amount of money in the program's budget for PW-PBIS, the ratio of behavioral consultants to children who require individualized support, and the number of PW-PBIS training sessions implemented. Data collection procedures must consider the structure of early childhood classrooms and use alternatives to teachers' personal record keeping if they are to be sustained. Because preschool teachers often have competing demands on their limited time, designating someone else in the early childhood program to organize and input child, teacher, classroom, and system-level data is advised.

In addition to the establishment of a PW-PBIS leadership team and the commitment to ongoing data collection and review, alternate forms of program support are necessary. It is essential to establish and maintain strong administrative support and active involvement of teachers. Before PW-PBIS may be implemented, it is important to secure the endorsement of the program's administrator (e.g., preschool director, school principal). At least 80% of teachers need to be in agreement with PW-PBIS implementation (also referred to as "teacher buy-in") within any given early childhood program prior to beginning assessment and professional development (Horner & Sugai, 2000). Program support is also important in providing regular professional development opportunities for program staff. Professional development opportunities should include workshops for learning new skills with classroom-based coaching to support teachers' translation of newly learned skills into their current teaching practices and sustained PW-PBIS implementation (Carter & Van Norman, 2010). Additional program support efforts to improve the success of PW-PBIS may include the following:

1. Providing staff with adequate time for lesson planning purposes either before the school day, during a break designated specifically for planning purposes, or after school

2. Maintaining adequate staffing levels, especially during challenging parts of the day

3. Providing staff with adequate resources (e.g., poster board) for creating materials related to PW-PBIS efforts

4. Providing positive reinforcement or acknowledgment of staff who implement PW-PBIS strategies successfully

An example of a staff acknowledgment system is provided in Figure 2.13.

- PW-PBIS team members nominate program employees implementing positive behavior supports on a secret ballot.

- Ballots are then anonymously entered into a monthly raffle.

- Names are drawn monthly and ballots are returned to those nominated for recognition.

- Sample prizes: donated gift cards, flowers, teaching supplies, special parking spot, extra planning time, extra break, and so forth.

Figure 2.13.   Staff acknowledgment system.

CHAPTER 3

Preparing for and Conducting the PreSET

FEATURES OF THE PreSET

The PreSET assesses classroom and program-wide variables across eight categories related to the primary/universal features of PW-PBIS:

1. Expectations Defined
2. Behavioral Expectations Taught
3. Responses to Appropriate and Challenging Behavior
4. Organized and Predictable Environment
5. Monitoring and Decision Making
6. Family Involvement
7. Management
8. Program Support

OVERVIEW OF PreSET ADMINISTRATION

Implementation of the PreSET first involves an interview with the program administrator using the PreSET Administrator Interview Form, as well as the collection and later review of program products (e.g., program handbook, classroom lesson plans, written communication to families). This interview takes approximately 15–20 minutes. Next, observations of and interviews with the lead teacher, other staff, and a sampling of children are conducted in each classroom in the early childhood program. Information obtained from observations and interviews in each classroom are documented on the PreSET Classroom Interview and Observation Form. One PreSET Classroom Interview and Observation Form should be completed for each classroom in the early childhood program. The evaluator will spend approximately 15–20 minutes in each classroom completing the PreSET Classroom Interview and Observation Form. Note that the PreSET classroom observation includes a specific observation of a transition period (under the Transition column) from an unstructured or less structured activity (e.g., free play, outdoor play) to a more structured activity (e.g., circle time, snack time) in each classroom. Knowledge of each classroom's key transitional times will help the evaluator to schedule observation times accordingly in each classroom.

Once interview and observation information is collected in each classroom, classroom scores are summarized on the PreSET Classroom Summary Form. Then, scores from the PreSET Classroom Summary Form and PreSET Administrator Interview Form are transferred to the PreSET Scoring Guide to calculate the program's implementation of PW-PBIS by feature and the program's total PreSET score.

A percent-implemented score is obtained for each of the eight subscales measured by the PreSET: Expectations Defined, Behavioral Expectations Taught, Responses to Appropriate and Challenging Behavior, Organized and Predictable Environment, Monitoring and Decision Making, Family Involvement, Management, and Program Support.

The percent-implemented score for each subscale is calculated by dividing the total points obtained for the subscale by the total points possible. For example, a program might obtain 8 points for items within the subscale Organized and Predictable Environment. There are 10 points possible for this subscale. So, the percent implemented for this subscale would be 80%. A total percent implemented is calculated by averaging all subscale scores. All percent-implemented scores are totaled and then divided by 8, resulting in an average percent-implemented score for the program.

ESTABLISHING RELIABILITY WITH THE PreSET

We highly recommend that individuals who conduct the PreSET be trained prior to administering the tool on their own. PreSET training can be conducted in either 1 full day or 2 half days, with approximately 6 hours of total training time during the initial training on PreSET administration. PreSET training involves a Microsoft PowerPoint presentation with information and photographic examples of PreSET items that were implemented in an early childhood center. Two case studies are provided to participants, one for practice and one for testing reliability in scoring. We also highly recommend field practice, in which participants independently administer a PreSET in an early childhood program and report their results back to their trainer within 4 weeks of the initial training.

To successfully complete PreSET training, attendees to the initial training attain reliability in administering and scoring the PreSET and complete a field practice component. Reliability is defined as at least 85% agreement in scoring for each item on the PreSET Scoring Guide during the final case study administered during the initial training session. If an attendee does not meet reliability with the case study, an action plan will be generated for the individual to obtain further training on necessary aspects of the administration or scoring process and to redo the case study at a later date. It is recommended that trained PreSET users maintain their reliability in administration and scoring by completing a PreSET with another trained individual at least once every 3 years.

A certified PreSET trainer conducts all training that is recommended for users of the PreSET. Individuals who are likely PreSET users, including early childhood behavioral consultants, behavioral support teachers, inclusion specialists, program administrators, and researchers or evaluators in the area of early childhood positive behavior support, should, if possible, participate in PreSET training. Users of the PreSET should not be employed or work in the center or program in which they are completing the assessment. They should have a neutral and external relationship with the center. They may be familiar with the program and have a previous and/or continuous relationship (e.g., consultant) with center staff, but they should not work full time in the center (e.g., a teacher or center director).

Individuals may become trained users of the PreSET through local trainings in their area. Individuals may also become certified PreSET trainers by completing the PreSET Train the Trainers program. To obtain more information on PreSET training for users or the PreSET Train the Trainers program, please visit Brookes on Location at http://www.brookespublishing.com/onlocation/index.htm.

PreSET ADMINISTRATION AND PROGRAM SIZE

It is recommended that PreSET administration follow the guidelines described in this manual in all programs, regardless of size. However, the authors recognize that there is an increase in the time and resources required to administer the PreSET as the size of the program increases. The classroom interview and observation takes approximately 15–20 minutes to complete in each program's classroom. Therefore, the amount of time for PreSET administration will increase with the number of classrooms in a program. Two or more evaluators may be required to administer the PreSET in a preschool center with more than 10 classrooms in one program day.

Evaluators may encounter a need to conduct the PreSET in a sample of classrooms rather than in all classrooms because of very large program size (e.g., more than 10 classrooms), inadequate evaluation resources (e.g., number of evaluators, evaluator time), or resistance on the part of the program to have all classrooms participate in the PreSET. When conducting the PreSET with a sample of classrooms, it is recommended that at least half of classrooms participate in the PreSET in order to gather an adequate amount of information and provide as accurate a program-wide implementation score as possible. The sample of classrooms should be selected at random by the evaluator(s) from a list of classrooms in the program. If there are varying types of classrooms in the program (e.g., by age or length of school day), the evaluator should ensure that a representative number of the varying types of classrooms are included in the sample.

CONTACTING THE PROGRAM

The individual conducting the PreSET should initiate communication with relevant preschool personnel by e-mail, phone, or in person to schedule the assessment. The contact person(s) may be administrators (e.g., preschool director, Head Start regional manager), relevant staff (e.g., family liaison), or teachers in the classroom. The choice of contact person should be made based on the program's organization of employees, size, and familiarity with the PreSET and the individual conducting the PreSET.

When contacting individuals at the preschool, the PreSET evaluator should explain the purpose of the assessment and how the results will benefit the program, staff, children, and families. Emphasis should be placed on how the information may help reduce and prevent children's challenging behavior and increase children's social-emotional skills. The administrator should also be told about the materials that he or she should ideally prepare in advance of the visit. The list of materials is presented on the Administrator Interview Form. It is important that administrators know that they are not expected to have all (or any) of these items. The evaluator will only wish to review these materials if they have been developed. The activities required of the teachers and children during the PreSET should also be explained during the initial contact with the program administrator. This information is described in the following section.

WHAT ADMINISTRATORS, TEACHERS, AND CHILDREN CAN EXPECT FROM THE PreSET

Program administrators will be interviewed using the PreSET Administrator Interview Form; this one-to-one interview will take approximately 15–20 minutes to complete. The specific arrangements for interviewing the program administrator should be made when initial contact and scheduling of the PreSET occurs. For ease of administration and scoring, it is highly recommended that the administrator interview occur prior to the classroom observations and staff/child interviews in order to ascertain whether staff responses match administrator responses on specific indicated questions. The evaluator will next observe and conduct interviews with the lead teacher, staff, and a sampling of children in each classroom. The PreSET Classroom Interview and Observation Form is provided for making notes during the classroom interviews with teachers and children and observations of specific classroom activities and materials.

As part of the evaluator's visit to each classroom, he or she will interview the lead teacher and other staff. The lead teacher will be asked questions about classroom organization, assessments, materials, and instructional strategies used in his or her classroom. This interview will take approximately 10 minutes and should ideally occur outside of regular classroom activities (e.g., during a break or while a substitute teacher takes over). The specific arrangement for interviewing the lead teacher should be made when initial contact and scheduling of the PreSET occurs. However, it is not necessary for classroom staff to leave the classroom during the interview, which would pose a staffing difficulty for programs in terms of maintaining adequate staff-to-child ratios and also disturb the flow of the environment. The evaluator is encouraged to briefly interview staff while completing the classroom observation within the environment, when appropriate, to alleviate scheduling concerns. Interviews of staff should occur at natural times during the classroom schedule that do not adversely affect or interfere with direct instruction (e.g., avoid circle time or other large group activities). It is also imperative to be aware of the teacher's primary responsibility to the safety of the children during all interviews. Other classroom teachers will be interviewed briefly (e.g., about 1–2 minutes) about classroom routines.

Finally, the evaluator will ask a teacher in the classroom to informally interview three children. The teacher may choose the children and will ask them brief and simple questions about their classroom (e.g., what they do after circle time). It is recommended that teachers ask the children the questions rather than the evaluator; this increases the likelihood that the children will respond to the questions and answer them accurately. Any necessary language adaptations (e.g., communication boards, assistive communication devices, gestural responses) should be used during the interviews with the children. Children should also be asked questions in their primary language during the interviews. The interviews with assistant teachers and children may easily be conducted during regular classroom activities.

The classroom observation will last approximately 10 minutes, including at least one play period (e.g., free play, discovery time, centers) and at least one transition from play to a more structured activity (e.g., circle time, a snack or meal). In addition to observing teacher–child interactions, the evaluator will note the presence and status of classroom materials related to PW-PBIS, including the following:

1. Program handbook
2. Behavior expectations/matrix
3. Lesson plans or cool tools documenting the teaching of the classroom expectations for each classroom implementing PW-PBIS (ideally seeking evidence that the classroom rules were directly taught to the children more than once in each classroom)
4. Acknowledgment/reinforcement plan
5. Behavior incident flow chart
6. Behavior incident report form or another data collection form that documents children's challenging behavior daily
7. PW-PBIS action plan
8. Written communication to families regarding PW-PBIS strategies in the classroom (e.g., newsletters, memos, announcements)

It is important to note that many preschool classrooms may not have developed these materials yet. Every attempt should be made to assure administrators and/or classroom teachers that they are not expected to have all of these materials, especially if the PreSET is being conducted prior to PW-PBIS implementation.

SCHEDULING THE PreSET

When scheduling the PreSET, arrange a time that accommodates the administrator's schedule for an interview and the program's schedule (e.g., no field trips, special events, other visitors). When observing in each classroom, plan to observe at least one play period and at least one transition from play to a more structured activity for each classroom; also plan time to interview the lead teacher(s), ideally outside of regular classroom activities. If the lead teacher is not immediately able to decide on a time to interview, the person scheduling the PreSET should help the teacher to problem solve to find a time in the day, resources (e.g., additional staff), or reorganization of staff (e.g., transfer of lead teacher duties to an assistant teacher) to be able to participate in the interview outside of the classroom.

CHAPTER 4

Collecting the Information

This chapter provides details about the guides and forms used to collect PreSET information.

PreSET ADMINISTRATOR INTERVIEW FORM

The PreSET Administrator Interview Form is used to collect information during the interview with the program administrator. The evaluator will ask the administrator information about the following:

1. Data on program or program characteristics (e.g., type of program, hours of operation)
2. Data on individual classrooms, including demographic information (e.g., number of staff, number of children)
3. How behavioral expectations are defined and taught at the program level
4. How the program has established guidelines to respond to appropriate and challenging behaviors
5. The program's data management systems to monitor children's challenging behavior and make decisions
6. Family involvement in PW-PBIS
7. Whether the program has established a team to address PW-PBIS; if so, how the team functions and the time and resources provided by the program to support PW-PBIS goals

Questions on the PreSET Administrator Interview Form are in the form of yes/no, multiple-choice, fill-in-the-blank, and open-ended questions. Each question that involves information to be transferred to the PreSET Scoring Guide includes the feature and item number located next to the question. A completed example page of the PreSET Administrator Interview Form is provided in Figure 4.1.

PreSET CLASSROOM INTERVIEW AND OBSERVATION FORM

The evaluator should use the PreSET Classroom Interview and Observation Form to record information during each classroom interview and observation. One form should be completed for each classroom. The form is organized by the following categories:

1. Staff questions (including lead teacher)
2. Student questions, including brief directions for interviewing children
3. Lead teacher questions
4. Classroom environment
5. The 10-minute classroom observation
6. Transition

V. Behavioral Expectations Defined and Taught (Features A and B)

A1	Has the program agreed to five or fewer positively stated expectations that are posted and the same for each classroom? (*Note: If the answer is "no" to A1, you may skip to "VI. Responses to Appropriate and Challenging Behavior" [Feature C].*)	No	Yes, but more than five, negatively stated, and/or classrooms have their own expectations	(Yes)
Use answer to corroborate teachers' responses during classroom interview (**B2**)	(If the program has rules) What are the rules?	*Be safe, be friendly, be helpful*		
Use answer to corroborate teachers' responses during classroom interview (**B1**)	(If the program has rules) How are the program's rules taught in each classroom?	*The rules are reviewed during story time by singing the rules song 2–3 times per week.*		
Notes: *Behavioral Expectations Defined and Taught (Features A and B):*		*The program rules are used in all classrooms; classroom 2 has a new lead teacher who may not be completely familiar with all the program components yet.*		

"Now I'd like to ask you about how the children know that they are meeting expectations…"

VI. Responses to Appropriate and Challenging Behavior (Feature C)

C1	Is there a system for acknowledging children's appropriate behavior that is frequently used in each classroom (e.g., special spotlight or raffle during circle, tokens for children who clean up after discovery)? (If yes) How often is it implemented? (*Note: If the answer is "no" to C1, you may skip to C3.*)	No	Yes, implemented once a day	Yes, implemented more than once a day

Figure 4.1. A completed example page of the PreSET Administrator Interview Form.

Notes are to be taken directly on this form during the interview and observation. After information is obtained, the evaluator scores each item with a yes or no using the criteria provided on the form. A completed example page of the PreSET Classroom Interview and Observation Form is provided in Figure 4.2.

PreSET CLASSROOM SUMMARY FORM

Classroom data collected on each PreSET Classroom Interview and Observation Form are transferred over to the PreSET Classroom Summary Form. There are 10 lines for 10 classrooms' data. However, if there are only three classrooms in the program, only three lines will be completed on the form. Multiple summary forms should be used if a program is larger than 10 classrooms. There is a summary line on the bottom of the form to tabulate the following scores for each item:

0: No classrooms are implementing the item

1: Half or less than half (but more than zero) of classrooms are implementing the item

2: The majority of classrooms are implementing the item

A completed example of the PreSET Classroom Summary Form is provided in Figure 4.3.

PreSET SCORING GUIDE

The PreSET Scoring Guide is used to aggregate information obtained from the PreSET Administrator Interview Form and PreSET Classroom Summary Form. The PreSET Scoring Guide includes eight primary/universal features of PW-PBIS:

1. Expectations Defined
2. Behavioral Expectations Taught
3. Responses to Appropriate and Challenging Behavior
4. Organized and Predictable Environment
5. Monitoring and Decision Making
6. Family Involvement
7. Management
8. Program Support

The Data Source column indicates the form from which the information should be transferred for each item (i.e., Administrator Interview Form, Classroom Summary Form). The PreSET Scoring Guide includes a section to compute summary scores for the program by feature and for the total percent implemented for all features. A completed example of the PreSET Scoring Guide, consisting of the last page with a scoring sample, is provided in Figure 4.4.

Program: __Early Childhood Program__   Classroom: __2- to 4-year olds__   Date: __March 9, 2011__

Teacher Questions
Interview up to three teachers

Respondent:	What are the program's rules? (B2) Record number known that match program's rules (Note: Automatically circle "no" if no program rules established.)		What happens after (circle time)? (D2) Must agree with posted classroom schedule and each other. Record + or –
	Number Known	Number of Rules	
Teacher 1	3	3	+
Teacher 2	3	3	+
Teacher 3			
Scoring	Did all interviewed teachers state the majority of the program rules? (Yes) No		Did all interviewed teachers correctly state what happens after (circle time)? (Yes) No

Children's Questions
A teacher should ask three children the following two questions. Use verbal prompting and accommodations for children's language abilities as necessary.

Respondent:	What are the rules in your classroom? (B3) Record number known that match program's rules (Note: Automatically circle "no" if no program rules established.)		What happens after (circle time)? (D3) Must agree with posted classroom schedule and teachers. Record + or –
	Number Known	Number of Rules	
Child 1	3	3	+
Child 2	2	3	+
Child 3	2	3	–
Scoring	Did all interviewed children state the majority of the classroom rules? (Yes) No		Did all interviewed children correctly state what happens after (circle time)? (Yes) No

Lead Teacher Questions

How do you teach the program rules in your classroom? (B1) (Note: Automatically circle "no" if no program rules established.)	How do you acknowledge appropriate behavior? (C2) (Note: Automatically circle "no" if no system identified by administrator.)	How do you respond to challenging behavior? (C4) (Note: Automatically circle "no" if no procedure identified by administrator.)	What do you use to collect data on children's challenging behavior? (E2) (Note: Automatically circle "no" if no data form identified by administrator.)	How do you communicate with families? (F1)	How do families participate in the classroom? (F2)	(If there is a PBIS team) What is the function of the program's PBIS team? (G2) (Note: Automatically circle "no" if no program-wide PBIS team established.)	Do you have sufficient time for planning and enough resources to meet your teaching goals? (H4)
Sing song at circle group activities	No system identified	No response procedure identified	No data form used	E-mail, newsletters, conferences	Read books, field trip volunteers	No team established	Yes
Program rules are taught in large or small groups? (Yes)* No *Must see a lesson plan to score "yes"	Is there a system? Yes* (No) *The system must match the program's and you must observe its use or evidence of its use to score "yes"	Is there a procedure? Yes* (No) *The procedure must match the program's and you must observe its use or evidence of its use to score "yes"	Data collection form? Yes* (No) *The form must match the program's form and you must observe its use or evidence of its use to score "yes"	Communicate with families? (Yes)* No *Must include at least one other way besides pick up and drop off to score "yes" (e.g., e-mail, phone, home visits)	Families participate in the classroom (e.g., classroom helpers, readers)? (Yes) No	(If there is a PBIS team) Correct function of the PW-PBIS team? Yes (No)	Sufficient planning time and adequate resources? (Yes) No

Figure 4.2.   A completed example page of the PreSET Classroom Interview and Observation Form.

Classroom Summary Form

Instructions: For a given program, transfer each classroom's scores from the Classroom Interview and Observation Form. Note the score as Y (yes) or N (no). When all participating classrooms' scores are transferred, complete the summary indicating a *0*, *1*, or *2* score.

Classroom	Teachers state rules (B2)	Teachers state what happens next (D2)	Children state rules (B3)	Children state what happens next (D3)	Plan to teach classroom rules (B1)	System to acknowledge appropriate behavior (C2)	System for responding to challenging behavior (C4)	Data collection form (E2)	Communicate with families in at least one way in addition to drop off/pick up (F1)	Families participate in classroom (F2)	Correct function of PW-PBIS team (G2)	Sufficient time and access to resources (H4)	Rules posted at eye level (A2)	Rules include words and visuals (A3)	Matrix of classroom rules (A4)	Schedule with visual pictures at eye level (D1)	Ratio of 4:1 positive to negative statements (C5)	Specific verbal praise (C6)	Precorrection during transition (C7)	Transition signal (D4)	Notice before transition signal (D5)
Classroom 1	Y	Y	Y	Y	Y	N	N	N	Y	Y	N	Y	N	Y	N	N	Y	Y	N	N	Y
Classroom 2	N	Y	N	Y	N	N	N	N	Y	N	Y	Y	Y	Y	N	Y	N	Y	Y	Y	Y
Classroom 3	Y	Y	Y	Y	Y	N	N	N	Y	N	N	Y	Y	Y	N	Y	Y	Y	N	N	Y
Classroom 4																					
Classroom 5																					
Classroom 6																					
Classroom 7																					
Classroom 8																					
Classroom 9																					
Classroom 10																					
Summary: (*0* = No for all; *1* = Yes for half or less than half; *2* = Yes for majority)	2	2	2	2	2	0	0	0	2	1	1	2	2	2	0	2	2	2	1	1	2
	B2	D2	B3	D3	B1	C2	C4	E2	F1	F2	G2	H4	A2	A3	A4	D1	C5	C6	C7	D4	D5

Figure 4.3. A completed example of the PreSET Classroom Summary Form.

35

PreSET

Feature	Evaluation question	Data source	Score (0, 1, 2)
H. Program Support	1. Does the program have a budget with sufficient funds for building and maintaining PW-PBIS? (0 = no; 1 = budget established, but insufficient funds; 2 = yes)	Administrator Interview Form	2
	2. Do program administrators report providing teachers with the time and resources (e.g., time to plan teaching lessons, money for rules posters) to implement goals related to PW-PBIS? (0 = no; 1 = limited planning time or resources; 2 = yes)	Administrator Interview Form	1
	3. Has there been at least one recent professional development opportunity for staff related to PW-PBIS? (0 = no; 1 = yes, but it was over a year ago; 2 = yes)	Administrator Interview Form	0
	4. Do teachers report having sufficient time and access to resources to implement goals related to PW-PBIS? (0 = no; 1 = half or less than half; 2 = majority of teachers)	Classroom Summary Form	1

PreSET program summary scores

Summary Scores	A Expectations Defined	B Behavioral Expectations Taught	C Responses to Appropriate and Challenging Behavior	D Organized and Predictable Environment	E Monitoring and Decision Making	F Family Involvement	G Management	H Program Support
	6 / 8	4 / 6	7 / 14	10 / 10	0 / 8	10 / 10	0 / 12	4 / 8
Percent implemented	75%	67%	50%	100%	0%	100%	0%	50%

Total percent implemented all features: 442   ÷ 8 =   55 %   (Average percent implemented)

Figure 4.4.   A completed example of the PreSET Scoring Guide.

CHAPTER 5

Scoring the PreSET

During PreSET administration, evaluators should make notes and answer all questions on the PreSET Administrator Interview Form and PreSET Classroom Interview and Observation Form. Evaluators should use the criteria to answer all questions on these forms. Evaluators should also take notes on the forms under and next to items about the specific information provided by the administrator, teachers, children, and observation. An example of how to take notes is provided in Figure 5.1, using the second page of the PreSET Classroom Interview and Observation Form. Once PreSET administration is completed with the administrator and all classrooms, evaluators should conduct the following scoring procedures at a separate location, such as their office.

The first step of scoring a program's PreSET involves transferring each classroom's scores from the Classroom Interview and Observation Form to a line on the PreSET Classroom Summary Form. For each feature of PW-PBIS on the top of the PreSET Classroom Summary Form (e.g., plan to teach classroom rules), the evaluator should transfer scores from the classroom's PreSET Classroom Interview and Observation Form in the form of a Y for *yes* or N for *no*. Evaluators should note that the letter and number notation of the features on the top of the PreSET Classroom Summary Form match the letter and numbers of items on the PreSET Classroom Interview and Observation Form to make transfer of data easier. An example of how to transfer the scores by matching the corresponding letters and numbers from the PreSET Classroom Interview and Observation Form to the PreSET Classroom Summary Form is provided in Figure 5.2.

After each classroom's data are transferred onto the PreSET Classroom Summary Form, the evaluators should complete the summary scoring information at the bottom of the PreSET Classroom Summary Form. Evaluators should give a score of *0, 1,* or *2* for each item on the PreSET Scoring Guide using information from the PreSET Administrator Interview Form and the PreSET Classroom Summary Form. Finally, evaluators should complete the summary scores at the end of the PreSET Scoring Guide, which provides summary scores for each PreSET category as well as an average percentage of features implemented for the program.

An opportunity to practice scoring the PreSET is included in this manual for a hypothetical early childhood program, the Busy Bee Preschool, in the case study in Appendix A. An answer key is provided for you to check your scoring and see an example of completed PreSET scoring materials.

The PreSET CD-ROM (sold separately) includes helpful Excel spreadsheets that are readymade for inputting, summarizing, and charting PreSET data. Once the user has entered PreSET data, the Excel forms automatically compute the percent implemented for each of the eight PreSET features as well as the total average percent implemented. These Excel forms also allow users to easily produce graphs to visually track universal PW-PBIS implementation year to year.

Classroom Environment

Use the items in italics to score the presence or absence of the following items in the classroom. (*Note: Automatically circle "no" for A2, A3, and A4 if no program rules established.*)

Are program rules posted in at least one classroom location at eye level? *Wall poster(s) (A2)*	Do program rules include a combination of words and visuals? *Wall poster(s) (A3)*	Are program rules incorporated into a matrix of expectations for classroom routines? *Matrix of classroom rules (A4)*	Is there a posted classroom schedule that includes visual pictures at eye level for children on at least one wall? *Classroom schedule (D1)*
(Yes) No	Yes (No)	Yes No	Yes (No)

10-minute Classroom Observation

Observe during a classroom routine such as free play, circle time, or snack; choose one teacher to observe.
Time started: __9:30 am__   Time ended: __9:40 am__

Tally the number of positive statements (praise, approval) (C5)	Tally the number of negative statements (reprimand, correction, disapproval) (C5)	Tally the number of comments using specific vebal praise (C6)
////	//	//

Divide the number of positive statements by the number of negative statements:

__4__ / __2__ = __2__

Is the result a number of 4.0 or greater?   Yes (No)

Was there at least 1?   (Yes) No

Transition

Observe at least one transition from an unstructured or less structured activity (e.g., free play, outside) to a more structured activity (e.g., circle time, snack time).

Did at least one teacher use pre-correction (e.g., remind a child of a classroom rule in the absence of misbehavior) at least once? (C7)	Did at least one teacher use a system other than or in addition to a verbal direction to signal the transition (e.g., ring bell, hand motion, sing song)? (D4)	Did at least one teacher provide a notice before the transition signal (e.g., play time over in 2 minutes)? (D5)
(Yes) No	(Yes) No	(Yes) No

Notes:

Specific verbal praise: "I saw you share that toy when Jacob asked you to play—great job being a good friend!"

"You were so helpful when you cleared up the toys you were using."

Pre-correction: "Please remember to wave quietly through the hallway."

Transition Signal: Train Whistle

Notice: 5-minute verbal warning provided

Figure 5.1. An example of how to take notes using the second page of the PreSET Classroom Interview and Observation Form.

PreSET — Lead Teacher Questions

How do you teach the program rules in your classroom? (B1) (Note: Automatically circle *"no"* if no program rules established.)	How do you acknowledge appropriate behavior? (C2) (Note: Automatically circle *"no"* if no system identified by administrator.)	How do you respond to challenging behavior? (C4) (Note: Automatically circle *"no"* if no procedure identified by administrator.)	What do you use to collect data on children's challenging behavior? (E2) (Note: Automatically circle *"no"* if no data form identified by administrator.)	How do you communicate with families? (F1)	How do families participate in the classroom? (F2)	(If there is a PBIS team) What is the function of the program's PBIS team? (G2) (Note: Automatically circle *"no"* if no program-wide PBS team established.)	Do you have sufficient time for planning and enough resources to meet your teaching goals? (H4)
Sing song at circle group activities	No system identified.	No response procedure identified	No data form used	E-mail, newsletters, conferences	Read books, field trip volunteers	No team established	Yes
Program rules are taught in large or small groups? (Yes)* No *Must see a lesson plan to score "yes"	Is there a system? Yes* (No) *The system must match the program's and you must observe its use or evidence of its use to score "yes"	Is there a procedure? Yes* (No) *The procedure must match the program's and you must observe its use or evidence of its use to score "yes"	Data collection form? Yes* (No) *The form must match the program's form and you must observe its use or evidence of its use to score "yes"	Communicate with families? (Yes) No *Must include at least one other way besides pick up and drop off to score "yes" (e.g., e-mail, phone, home visit)	Families participate in the classroom (e.g., classroom helpers, readers)? (Yes) No	(If there is a PBIS team) Correct function of the PW-PBIS team? Yes (No)	Sufficient planning time *and* adequate resources? (Yes) No

Classroom Summary Form

Instructions: For a given program, transfer each classroom's scores from the Classroom Interview and Observation Form. Note the score as Y (yes) or N (no). When all participating classrooms' scores are transferred, complete the summary indicating a 0, 1, or 2 score.

Classroom	Teachers state rules (B2)	Teachers state what happens next (D2)	Children state rules (B3)	Children state what happens next (D3)	Plan to teach classroom rules (B1)	System to acknowledge appropriate behavior (C2)	System for responding to challenging behavior (C4)	Data collection form (E2)	Communicate with families in at least one way in addition to drop of/pick up (F1)	Families participate in classroom (F2)	Correct function of PW-PBIS team (G2)	Sufficient time and access to resources (H4)	Rules posted at eye level (A2)	Rules include words and visuals (A3)	Matrix of classroom rules (A4)	Schedule with visual pictures at eye level (D1)	Ratio of 4:1 positive to negative statements (C5)	Specific verbal praise (C6)	Precorrection during transition (C7)	Transition signal (D4)	Notice before transition signal (D5)
Classroom 1					Y	N	N	N	Y	Y	N	Y									

Figure 5.2. An example of how to transfer the scores by matching the corresponding letters and numbers from the PreSET Classroom Interview and Observation Form to the PreSET Classroom Summary Form.

CHAPTER 6

Interpreting and Sharing PreSET Results

INTERPRETING THE RESULTS

Once a program's scoring materials are complete and the PreSET Scoring Guide is scored, evaluators will need to communicate the scores to relevant program staff and/or PW-PBIS team members. Scores may be interpreted and communicated at the program level, classroom level, or both.

To interpret program-level scores, the evaluator should use the percent implemented scores for each category and the average percent implemented to determine the percentage of features the program has in place at the time of PreSET administration. Programs that have not yet implemented PW-PBIS with trainings and coaching are likely to score less than 50% in each feature and for their average percent of features implemented. It is not uncommon for programs to score in the 10%–30% range upon first PreSET administration (Steed & Roach, 2011). Programs that are in their second year of PW-PBIS implementation with trainings and coaching are likely to score between 40% and 60% in each feature and for their average percent of features implemented. Programs are considered to be implementing PW-PBIS with fidelity when they implement at least 80% of items in Feature B (Behavioral Expectations Taught) and in their average percent of features implemented. These markers are general guidelines and are adopted from the literature on SW-PBIS.

Initial efforts in the area of PW-PBIS in early childhood settings indicate that it may take 2–3 years of intensive professional development (including ongoing classroom coaching) for a program to implement practices associated with PW-PBIS and/or the Teaching Pyramid (Fox, Hemmeter, Snyder, Binder, & Clarke, 2011). It is recommended that programs conduct the PreSET twice a year (fall and spring of an academic year) during the first few years of PW-PBIS implementation to monitor changes in their results that reflect classroom and program-wide improvements. Once the program obtains an average implementation of approximately 80%, they may choose to reduce PreSET administration to once a year (usually in the fall). A yearly PreSET in the fall will allow leadership teams to plan professional development and discuss program-wide goals to reach full implementation of PW-PBIS, as well as the critical task of maintaining the use of PW-PBIS already in place.

To interpret classroom-level scores, the evaluator should use each classroom's scores on the PreSET Classroom Summary Form. This form allows the evaluator to compare and contrast the individual features of PW-PBIS being implemented in each classroom within the program. The evaluator may also use this form to identify trends across classrooms, such as uniform practices across classrooms to communicate with families, or the evaluator may identify trends within a cluster of classrooms, such as a group of classrooms that are implementing classroom schedules or transition signals. This information can then be translated into specific recommendations and goals for lead classroom teachers and/or teaching teams within each classroom environment by means of individualized and informed professional development plans. For example, if a cluster of teachers has developed lesson plans to teach program-wide rules while other teachers have yet to do so, these developed lesson plans may be shared with all teachers to bolster program-wide adoption of teaching the behavioral expectations in all classrooms.

In another example, a program administrator may assume that all teachers are using a program-wide method of responding to children's challenging behavior. Analyses of the PreSET Classroom Summary Form may indicate inconsistent implementation of behavior management strategies across teachers. This finding would lead to professional development and/or other actions on the part of the leadership team and classroom teachers to improve their consistent use of agreed-on strategies to prevent and respond to children's challenging behavior. Furthermore, one teacher may have developed a unique and effective system for collecting and inputting data on children's challenging behavior that the teacher charts and shares with the classroom team and children's families. This finding may lead to a suggestion to use the teacher's system as a model for the program administrator and leadership team as they plan improvements to program-wide management of data related to children's challenging behavior.

SHARING THE RESULTS WITH PROGRAMS

Evaluators should share PreSET results with relevant program staff and/or a program's PW-PBIS leadership team in a timely fashion after PreSET results have been calculated (e.g., within 2 weeks). Results should ideally be shared in person during a meeting. If this is not possible, results may be shared by telephone and/or e-mail communication.

The evaluator should begin sharing results with the program staff by first reiterating the purpose of the PreSET, which is to measure implementation of features of PW-PBIS at the universal level of support. Program staff should also be reminded of the data collected and procedures used to collect the information, including an interview with the program administrator, interviews and observations in each classroom, and a review of permanent products (e.g., program handbook, lesson plans, newsletters to families).

Next, the evaluator should summarize the program's scores in each feature, going into more detail with examples of positive aspects of the program's implementation of PW-PBIS. For example, if some of the teachers' use of praise was especially noteworthy, the evaluator may provide specific feedback about this:

> Teachers in prekindergarten classrooms 2 and 4 were observed to use a ratio of approximately five positive statements, such as "Good for you" and "Nice job sharing," to each negative statement, such as "Stop doing that" and "No," that were directed at children. Research indicates that a 4:1 ratio is optimal to keep children positively engaged in social interactions and appropriate activities. The teachers in these classrooms exceeded that ratio, which is wonderful.

All areas of strength in which PreSET features are being implemented should be mentioned in the feedback report. Areas of improvement should be identified and communicated to program staff strategically. For example, if a program has relatively low PreSET scores (e.g., 10%–30% implementation) because it is their first PreSET, there may be too many areas of improvement to mention in the initial feedback to staff. Instead of listing all areas of improvement, the evaluator should choose areas for feedback that seem most in need and/or represent the program's priorities and goals. For example, if the program is especially interested in improving their collaborations with families and increasing their consistency of using specific prevention strategies across classrooms, these areas could be a focus of feedback over other areas in which the program is not ready to devote resources (e.g., developing a data management system or teaching behavioral expectations). It is often helpful to accompany suggestions with examples (e.g., a picture of a rules poster). Recommendations should be worded constructively so that programs may incorporate these suggestions into an action plan for future progress on implementing features of PW-PBIS.

EXAMPLE OF HOW TO SHARE PreSET RESULTS

An example of how to share PreSET results in a meeting with program staff is provided in the following sections. This information can also be shared using the Feedback Form, as shown in the sample form on page 48. A blank Feedback Form is included on the CD-ROM.

Preschool-Wide Evaluation Tool (PreSET) Feedback

Program: Morrow Heights Preschool   **Date of feedback:** 03/23/09

Administrator: Holly Jackson   **Date of PreSET:** 03/17/09–03/18/09

City, state: Vicksburg, GA   **Date of last PreSET:** Not applicable

Number of classrooms in program: 4

PreSET data collector(s): Rachel Isaacson and Andy Patel

PreSET Administration

The PreSET was administered during two mornings in the Morrow Heights Preschool. The PreSET included an interview with Holly Jackson, the program administrator, and interviews and observations in each of the four preschool classrooms. The PreSET data collectors were able to quickly and efficiently gather needed data due to the receptiveness, flexibility, and openness of the program staff.

Overview of PreSET Results

The Morrow Heights program is currently implementing many research-based practices related to supporting young children's social-emotional development. For example, some classrooms are using visual schedules of the classroom schedule to help children predict the order of routines in the classroom and what is happening next. To further assist with transitions from one routine to another, some classrooms are using transition signals, such as a song that is sung or lights that are turned off and on when it is time to clean up and make the transition to circle time. Some classroom teachers were observed to frequently acknowledge children's appropriate behavior and to use specific verbal praise (e.g., "thank you for raising your hand"). Of particular note across programs was the consistent and regular communication with families through telephone calls, e-mails, and notes sent home in children's backpacks. In addition, teachers felt supported with adequate time and access to resources for planning. Teachers repeatedly commented about the positive work environment in the program and their high job satisfaction.

Although many important strategies were observed during PreSET administration, other PW-PBIS strategies were identified as not yet implemented. It is important for Morrow Heights Preschool program staff to remember that these PreSET scores reflect baseline implementation of PW-PBIS strategies. These strategies may be implemented in individual classrooms and not on a program level at this time. Furthermore, there may be areas addressed on the PreSET that have not been previously identified as priorities for the Morrow Heights Preschool program. The PW-PBIS strategies not yet implemented included established classroom rules and expectations, classroom rules posters, plans to teach classroom rules and expectations, systems for acknowledging appropriate behavior and responding to challenging behavior, and data collection for addressing challenging behavior.

Feature A: Expectations Defined

The Morrow Heights Preschool program does not have program-wide rules and expectations identified at this time. Classroom teachers identified various rules for their classrooms, such as no running, hands to self, and be safe. There were no rules posters or teaching matrices in the Morrow Heights Preschool classrooms (see Figure 6.1).

Feature B: Behavioral Expectations Taught

The Morrow Heights Preschool program does not systematically teach classroom rules at this time. During observations in classrooms, many children engaged in appropriate classroom behavior (e.g., responded to teacher directions, used quiet voices indoors). However, there were occasions in which children did not follow typical classroom expectations (e.g., not following teacher directions, noncompliance, screaming, leaving the group activity, hitting other children). Children in the Morrow Heights Preschool program may benefit from ongoing instruction and support to engage in desired classroom behaviors.

Feature C: Responses to Appropriate and Challenging Behavior

The Morrow Heights Preschool program does not have an established system for acknowledging appropriate behavior (e.g., special spotlight for a child during circle time, raffle tickets for children who clean up after discovery time) or a system for responding to challenging behavior (e.g., restate classroom rule, removal from activity). Lead teachers did identify various strategies that they used to acknowledge appropriate behavior, such as verbal praise, hugs, and stickers. Lead teachers also identified strategies that were used to respond to challenging behavior, including verbal redirection.

Morrow Heights Preschool program teachers were observed to use frequent positive statements to children. No teachers were observed to use precorrection, in which they state an expected behavior before misbehavior occurs (see Figure 6.2).

If the Morrow Heights Preschool program wants to develop a system for acknowledging children's appropriate behavior, it is important that the system be developmentally appropriate for the preschoolers with and without disabilities in the program (i.e., the

Example of a rules poster	Example of a teaching matrix			
	Daily routines	**Take care of ourselves**	**Take care of each other**	**Take care of our things**
	Arrival	• Walk to our cubbies • Join play nicely	• Say hello to others	• Put things away
	Free play & outside	• Follow directions • Ask for help (if we need it)	• Join play nicely • Include others • Share • Take turns • Use our words	• Treat things safely • Put things away
	Circle	• Sit on mat • Participate	• Take turns • Follow directions • Keep hands and feet in spot	• Clear away mats • Hang up jobs
	Snack	• Follow directions • Face the table • Keep hands and feet in spot	• Use our manners • Answer others	• Put things away

Figure 6.1. Examples of a rules poster and a teaching matrix. (Photo by Howard S. Muscott, Ed.D., Director, New Hampshire Center for Effective Behavioral Intervention and Supports [NH CEBIS] at SERESC, Bedford; reprinted by permission.)

Classroom	Number of positive statements (e.g., praise, approval)	Number of negative statements (e.g., reprimand, correction, disapproval)	Ratio of positive to negative statements	Specific verbal praise used?	Precorrection used?
Jackie	8	4	2:1	Yes	No
Kyle	8	1	8:1	Yes	No
Rashion	20	4	5:1	Yes	No
Patti	18	4	4.5:1	No	No

Figure 6.2. Precorrection chart.

system should be simple and involve fairly immediate primary reinforcement). It is not recommended that any system for responding to challenging behavior use positive strategies exclusively (e.g., removal of reinforcement following challenging behavior). Ideally, the Morrow Heights Preschool program staff would decide on various procedures that are used in response to various challenging behaviors and then document these procedures (e.g., in a program handbook).

It would be beneficial for students receiving physical prompting in response to challenging behavior to receive more intensive programming regarding prevention of challenging behavior (e.g., identifying problem times and triggers), if this has not been done already. It is also important that these children be taught replacement behaviors to attempt to decrease the use of physical prompting following challenging behavior.

Feature D: Organized and Predictable Environment

A classroom schedule with pictures was posted in three of the four classrooms. Classroom teachers were knowledgeable about the classroom routines and the order in which they occurred. Children were observed to move easily and efficiently from routine to routine in two classrooms. Some of the children in the other two classrooms required physical prompting to make the transition from one activity to the next. The Morrow Heights Preschool program should be acknowledged for its use of visual schedules in its classrooms. Overall, children appeared to know what to expect from their day. Those classrooms in which children required physical prompting to make the transition from one activity to the next may consider using a visual schedule and transition signals, which are being used in other classrooms.

Feature E: Monitoring and Decision Making

The Morrow Heights Preschool program does not collect data on children's challenging behavior at this time. A sample data collection form will be shared with program staff to provide an example of how the program might do this in the future.

Feature F: Family Involvement

The Morrow Heights Preschool program appears to communicate regularly and consistently with children's families through daily notes home to families in children's backpacks, as well as telephone calls, e-mails, and face-to-face communication during pick-up and drop-off with individual children's families. The program does not involve or notify families of PW-PBIS strategies (e.g., classroom rules, approach to challenging behavior) at this time. It is advisable for the Morrow Heights Preschool program to provide this information to families through the program handbook or other communication with families (e.g., newsletter, materials presented to families at orientation).

Feature G: Management

The Morrow Heights Preschool program staff meets as a group once a month to discuss program issues and individual children, but does not specifically address PW-PBIS issues at this time. The group that attends these monthly meetings includes the program administrator, lead teachers, assistant teachers, speech-language pathologists, occupational therapists, and the special education nurse. Preschool teachers also meet informally each day for lunch.

If the Morrow Heights Preschool program would like to address more PW-PBIS in its program, it seems appropriate to add these items to the agenda for preschool team meetings, rather than setting up an additional team specific to PW-PBIS. (However, this decision is up to the program.) The identification of priorities and a plan for implementation of PW-PBIS (i.e., action plan) would be advised to guide planning during team meetings. An example of an action plan will be shared with program staff.

Feature H: Program Support

The Morrow Heights Preschool program appears to offer adequate time for staff to plan. The afternoons are used by teachers to plan classroom activities. Teachers are not currently using this time for planning for PW-PBIS specifically. There have not been any professional development opportunities related to PW-PBIS in the last year. However, professional development is a priority for the program in general. If the Morrow Heights Preschool program plans to implement more PW-PBIS, they should provide professional development to staff in the next academic year.

Conclusions

The Morrow Heights Preschool program is implementing many positive strategies and supports for the children in its preschool classrooms. Any PW-PBIS strategies that the Morrow Heights Preschool program identifies for future implementation are likely to succeed because of the strong and experienced staff, communication between staff, and support from the program administrator.

PreSET Summary Scores

PreSET summary scores for the Morrow Heights Preschool program are provided in Figure 6.3.

LINKING PreSET RESULTS TO PW-PBIS IMPROVEMENT

Once a preschool program's leadership team has met to review PreSET results, these data may be used to develop action plans toward PW-PBIS improvement. Prior to creating the action plan, teams should discuss their priorities, available resources, and the areas that were indicated as not yet implemented on the PreSET. The team should then choose three to five goals related to their PreSET results that they will address in the academic year. The chosen goals should match the program's priorities and available resources. Choosing realistic goals that the team is genuinely interested in tackling will increase their likelihood of success. Action plans may be outlined in team meeting minutes as goals or objectives that are monitored and updated during each team meeting. Alternatively, the team may choose to develop an action plan document that the team uses to chart its progress toward implementing PW-PBIS features. The PreSET PW-PBIS Action Plan is included on the PreSET CD-ROM.

PreSET

Summary scores	A Expectations Defined	B Behavioral Expectations Taught	C Responses to Appropriate and Challenging Behavior	D Organized and Predictable Environment	E Monitoring and Decision Making	F Family Involvement	G Management	H Program Support
	0 / 8	0 / 6	6 / 14	7 / 10	1 / 8	2 / 10	0 / 12	0 / 8
Percent imple-mented	0%	0%	43%	70%	13%	20%	0%	0%

Total percent imple-mented all features:

146 ÷ 8 = 18 % (Average percent implemented)

Figure 6.3   Sample summary scores from the PreSET Scoring Guide.

 **PreSET.** | **Feedback Form**

Preschool: _Morrow Heights_   Number of classrooms: _4_

District: _Vicksburg, GA_   Date of visit: _03/23/09_

PreSET evaluator: _Holly Jackson_

The Preschool-Wide Evaluation Tool™ (PreSET™) is an adaptation of an assessment tool known as the School-Wide Evaluation Tool (SET) used in kindergarten (K)–12 educational settings to measure critical features of schoolwide positive behavior intervention and support (SW-PBIS; Sugai, Lewis-Palmer, Todd, & Horner, 2001). Because of the distinct differences between K–12 and early childhood educational settings, the PreSET was developed to accurately assess and evaluate the implementation status of program-wide positive behavior intervention and support (PW-PBIS) in early childhood settings.

The PreSET includes some of the categories used in the SET (e.g., Expectations Defined, Behavioral Expectations Taught, Monitoring and Decision Making) as well as new categories (e.g., Organized and Predictable Environment, Family Involvement). The PreSET uses the identical 0–2 scoring system used when conducting the SET. Furthermore, the PreSET includes some items from the SET. Other items were modified or added to ensure that the instrument was suited to early childhood settings. All items included on the PreSET were informed by current research on PW-PBIS in early childhood settings and developmentally appropriate practice.

The PreSET assesses classroom and program-wide variables across eight categories related to primary/universal features of PW-PBIS:

A. Expectations Defined

B. Behavioral Expectations Taught

C. Responses to Appropriate and Challenging Behavior

D. Organized and Predictable Environment

E. Monitoring and Decision Making

F. Family Involvement

G. Management

H. Program Support

Each feature is computed as a percentage and then expressed as percent implemented. The following scoring requirements must be met for a program to be assessed as implementing an effective program-wide behavior support based on PBIS principles:

- *The total score is 80% or better.*

PreSET Evaluation Results

Discussion and recommendations

Features	Percent implemented
Expectations Defined	38%
Behavioral Expectations Taught	17%
Responses to Appropriate and Challenging Behavior	43%
Organized and Predictable Environment	100%
Monitoring and Decision Making	0%
Family Involvement	40%
Management	75%
Program Support	100%
Average of features score	52%

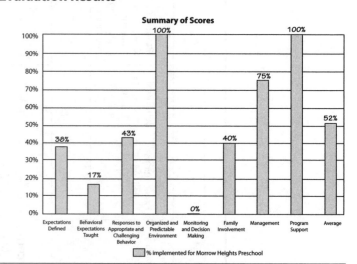

NOTE: These results are considered to be baseline data because the PreSET was completed prior to beginning PW-PBIS training and support. Expectations were that the scores for this evaluation would be low. Most elements are not expected to be in place at this point in the PW-PBIS training process.

FEATURE A. Expectations Defined

The Morrow Heights Preschool program does not have program-wide rules and expectations identified at this time. Classroom teachers identified various rules for their classrooms, such as, "no running," "hands to self," and "be safe." There were no rules, posters, or teaching matrices in the Morrow Heights Preschool classrooms.

FEATURE B. Behavioral Expectations Taught

The Morrow Heights Preschool program does not systematically teach classroom rules at this time. During observations in classrooms, many children engaged in appropriate classroom behavior (e.g., responded to teacher directions, used quiet voice indoors). However, there were occasions in which children did not follow typical classroom expectations (e.g., not following teacher directions, noncompliance, screaming, leaving the group activity, hitting other children). Children in the Morrow Heights Preschool program may benefit from ongoing instruction and support to engage in desired classroom behaviors.

FEATURE C. Responses to Appropriate and Challenging Behavior

The Morrow Heights Preschool program does not have an established system for acknowledging appropriate behavior (e.g., special spotlight for a child during circle, raffle tickets for children who clean up after discovery time) or a system for responding to challenging behavior (e.g., restate classroom rule, removal from activity). Lead teachers did identify various strategies that they used to acknowledge appropriate behavior, such as verbal praise, hugs, and stickers. Lead teachers also identified strategies that were used to respond to challenging behavior, including verbal redirection.

Morrow Heights Preschool program teachers were observed to use frequent positive statements to children. No teachers were observed to use pre-correction (stating an expected behavior before misbehavior occurs).

If the Morrow Heights Preschool program wants to develop a system for acknowledging children's appropriate behavior, it will be important that the system is developmentally appropriate for the preschoolers with and without disabilities in the program (i.e., the system should be simple and involve fairly immediate primary reinforcement). It is not recommended that any system for responding to challenging behavior use positive strategies exclusively (e.g., removal of reinforcement following challenging behavior). Ideally the Morrow Heights Preschool program staff would decide on various procedures that are used in response to various challenging behaviors and document these procedures (e.g., in a program handbook). It would be beneficial for students receiving physical prompting in response to challenging behavior to receive more intensive programming regarding prevention of challenging behavior (e.g., identifying problem times and triggers), if this has not been done already.

FEATURE D. Organized and Predictable Environment

A classroom schedule with pictures was posted in three of the four classrooms. Classroom teachers were knowledgeable about the classroom routines and the order in which they occurred. Children were observed to move easily and efficiently from routine to routine in two classrooms. Some of the children in the other two classrooms required physical prompting to transition from one activity to the next. The Morrow Heights Preschool program should be acknowledged for its use of visual schedules in its classrooms. Overall, children appeared to know what to expect from their day. Those classrooms in which children required physical prompting to transition from one activity to the next may consider using a visual schedule and transition signals that are being used in other classrooms.

FEATURE E. Monitoring and Decision Making

The Morrow Heights Preschool program does not collect data on children's challenging behavior at this time. A sample data collection form will be shared with program staff to provide an example of how the program might do this in the future.

FEATURE F. Family Involvement

The Morrow Heights Preschool program appears to communicate regularly and consistently with children's families through daily notes home to families in children's backpacks, as well as telephone calls, e-mails, and face-to-face communication during pick-up and drop-off with individual children's families. The program does not involve or notify families of PW-PBIS strategies (e.g., classroom rules, approach to challenging behavior) at this time. It is advisable for the Morrow Heights Preschool program to provide this information to families through the program handbook or other communication with families (e.g., newsletter, materials presented to families at orientation).

FEATURE G. Management

The Morrow Heights Preschool program staff meets as a group once a month to discuss program issues and individual children, but does not specifically address PW-PBIS issues at this time. The group that attends these monthly meetings includes the program administrator, lead teachers, assistant teachers, speech-language pathologists, occupational therapists, and the special education nurse. Preschool teachers also meet informally each day for lunch. If the Morrow Heights Preschool program would like to address more PW-PBIS in its program, it seems appropriate to add these items to the agenda for preschool team meetings, rather than setting up an additional team specific to PW-PBIS. (However, this decision is up to the program.) The identification of priorities and a plan for implementation of PW-PBIS (i.e., action plan) would be advised to guide planning during team meetings. An example of an action plan will be shared with program staff.

FEATURE H. Program Support

The Morrow Heights Preschool program appears to offer adequate time for staff to plan. The afternoons are used by teachers to plan classroom activities. Teachers are not currently using this time for planning for PW-PBIS specifically. There have not been any professional development opportunities related to PW-PBIS in the last year. However, professional development is a priority for the program in general. If the Morrow Heights Preschool program plans to implement more PW-PBIS, they should provide professional development to staff in the next academic year.

Average of features. The overall average score of __52__ % for this evaluation indicates that

The Morrow Heights Preschool program is implementing many positive strategies and supports for the children in its preschool classrooms. Any PW-PBIS strategies that the Morrow Heights Preschool program identifies for future implementation are likely to succeed because of the strong and experienced staff, communication between staff, and support from the program administrator.

Respectfully yours,

Holly Jackson

PreSET Evaluator

Case Study
The Busy Bee Preschool

The Busy Bee Preschool is a hypothetical full-day preschool program licensed to serve 60 children, inclusive of children with disabilities. The program receives child care scholarships from the state for children from low-income families. The program has three preschool classrooms. Preschool 1 is licensed for 16 children, serves 3- and 4-year-old children, and employs two staff members (a lead teacher and an assistant teacher). Preschool 2 is licensed for 18 children, is a multiage classroom serving 3- to 5-year-old children, and employs two staff members (a lead teacher and an assistant). Preschool 3 is the largest classroom; it serves 24 children ages 4–5 and employs three staff members (one lead teacher and two assistants). One preschool director is the administrator and owner for the Busy Bee Preschool.

The case study for the Busy Bee Preschool includes the following information in order to provide you with the opportunity to practice scoring the PreSET:

- Busy Bee Preschool Parent Handbook
- Completed PreSET Administrator Interview Form
- Notes on the PreSET Classroom Interview and Observation Form for each classroom

Use the case study information to complete the blank practice forms provided in this manual, as well as the following instructions:

1. Complete each classroom's PreSET Classroom Interview and Observation Form by circling *Yes* or *No* for each item on the forms.

2. Use the data provided and that you filled in on the three classrooms' PreSET Classroom Interview and Observation Forms to complete the blank PreSET Classroom Summary Form.

3. Use the data provided on the PreSET Administrator Interview Form and PreSET Classroom Summary Form to complete the blank PreSET Scoring Guide.

4. Check your answers on the case study practice forms with the answer keys provided at the end of Appendix A.

Busy Bee Parent Handbook

Dear Busy Bee Preschool Parent,

Welcome to the Busy Bee Preschool Program! We look forward to working with you and your child to provide a fun and educational experience. We are using an exciting program in all of our classrooms to promote healthy social skills and to manage children's behavior. We are participating in a statewide initiative—program-wide positive behavior intervention and support (PW-PBIS)—to create a program-wide system that will help children learn the skills they need to succeed in the classroom socially, emotionally, developmentally, and behaviorally. This handbook will explain how it will work and what you can expect your child to be learning. We are very excited about the way this will change our classrooms by making them more positive, more consistent, and more supportive. After looking through this handbook, if you have any questions about the program, please feel free to speak with the director. Together we can get your child off to a great start.

Sincerely,

The Busy Bee Preschool Team

> *Beatrice Smith*, Director of Busy Bee Preschool, PBIS Coach*
> *Miss Carter* and Miss Jones, Preschool 1 teachers*
> *Miss Valley* and Miss Greene, Preschool 2 teachers*
> *Miss Grant, Miss Jesse, and Mr. Bob,* Preschool 3 teachers*

*Indicates teachers who participate on the Positive Behavior Busy Bee Preschool Leadership team, along with a parent representative. If you are interested in joining our team for monthly meetings concerning the Busy Bee positive behavior curriculum, please contact the director. Parent participation is highly supported, valued, and appreciated!

Our Busy Bee buzz words

⬡ BE SAFE

⬡ BE KIND

⬡ BE HELPFUL

Busy Bee Positive Behavior Curriculum

The Busy Bee positive behavior curriculum was created by a team of Busy Bee employees and parents working together with funding from a state grant. Our team has attended training sessions with some of the leaders in the field of children's behavior. With the help of the statewide trainings and onsite support, we came up with the Busy Bee positive behavior curriculum, based on the following main ideas:

- Children need to know what is expected of them.
- Children need to be directly taught the correct way to behave.
- Correct behavior needs to be encouraged and acknowledged.
- There needs to be a consistent system for responding to challenging behavior.
- Data need to be collected, reviewed, and used to monitor progress and make decisions related to program improvement.

Children Need to Know What Is Expected of Them

To make things more consistent throughout Busy Bee Preschool and to make it easier for the children to know and follow the rules, we have come up with three main rules (referred to as *buzz words*) that will be used in all of our classrooms. They are easy for children to understand and for teachers to remember. The three Busy Bee buzz words are

 BE SAFE

 BE KIND

 BE HELPFUL

These rules allow us to address any behavior challenges that may occur in the classrooms and also help children learn how to be safe, respectful, and responsible in the classroom environment and in the community. You will see these rules posted in all of our classrooms and you will hear staff refer to the rules frequently throughout the day. Feel free to use these buzz words at home to address any behavioral challenges you may encounter with your child (see attached poster in Figure A.1 for home use). This helps in building a strong and positive home–school connection for children and families.

Children Need to Be Taught the Expectations

You may notice that our rules are very general and do not really explain how to be safe, be kind, or be helpful. This explanation will be provided using individual lessons in the classrooms (called *cool tools*). These short lessons will explain and define each rule for the children by further breaking them down into positively stated language. Our goal in doing this is to teach the children what they can do instead of always telling them what they can't or shouldn't do. For example, *Be safe* includes the buzz phrase to "use walking feet." See the behavior matrix in Figure A.2 for all of the buzz words and phrases associated with *Be safe, Be kind,* and *Be helpful* within each classroom routine.

Busy Bee Positive Behavior Curriculum

Our Busy Bee buzz words

⬡ BE SAFE

⬡ BE KIND

⬡ BE HELPFUL

Figure A.1. Poster of buzz words to convey behavioral expectations.

To teach children how to use walking feet, the teacher may explain why it is an important part of being safe. The children will be given specific examples of situations where walking will keep them safe; they also will take part in activities that will allow them to practice. Teachers will always show the children (model) what the correct behavior looks like so that the children become familiar with it. In this way, the children will have a very clear idea of the behaviors that are acceptable and expected in the classroom. Good teaching practices allow children the opportunity to see, hear, and do! In this way, children will listen and learn about the rules, and we will provide pictures and role modeling to further illustrate the rule or concept. We will incorporate fun songs, finger plays, flannel board stories, and/or puppets to teach the rules. The children will have opportunities to practice the rules, and they will be acknowledged for positive behavior as well!

The cool tools have been created by teachers and team members to teach behavior in any setting. It is important to teach the behavior where you want it to take place. For example, teaching safe playground behavior needs to be taught on the playground. The same is true for meals, circle time, and other parts of the child's day. In this way, children make the connection between the behavior and the setting.

Expectations Need to Be Encouraged and Acknowledged

Once a behavior is taught, a child must be motivated to use that behavior in place of less appropriate behavior. In the Busy Bee positive behavior curriculum, we accomplish this through positive feedback from caregivers. If a child is following the rules, a teacher may say, "I like the way you are being safe by walking to line up." This recognizes the child and lets the child see that others are aware that he or she is following the rules. Please notice that the recognition is very specific. The child was given more information than just "good job."

The staff will also provide frequent reminders and precorrections to help the children remember certain rules, especially during times of transition, which can be problematic and difficult for young children. For example, a teacher may say, "Before we go to the playground, remember we stay safe by using walking feet and staying in line." This helps the children to follow the rules by reminding them ahead of time instead of having to correct them after a behavioral mistake occurs.

An acknowledgment system will also be used to reinforce positive behaviors in the classroom. The Busy Bee acknowledgment system is based on every child collecting a token to work toward a group goal. Each child will be acknowledged with positive verbal

Busy Bee Buzz Words

	BE SAFE	BE KIND	BE HELPFUL
Free play/ choice time	• Use walking feet • Feet on the floor • Use gentle hands • Use our things carefully	• Share & care • Use kind words • Use inside voices • Take turns • Be a friend	• Use listening ears • Make happy choices • Clean up • Do your best
Circle/ group time	• Sit criss-cross applesauce • Keep hands and feet to self	• Leave space for others • Sit so everyone can see • Raise your hand	• Follow directions • Listen & look • Get involved
Meals/ snacks	• Wash your hands • Take small bites & chew slowly • Stay seated • Pass carefully	• Use good manners • Use inside voices • Use polite talking	• Set up • Clean up
Outdoor play	• Dress for the weather • Use listening ears • Use sand carefully • Wear helmets on bikes	• Take turns • Be aware • Include everyone • Work it out with words • Ask for help	• Keep the gate closed • Clean up
Bathroom	• Wash hands • Feet on the floor • Keep water in the sink	• Take turns • Knock before entering	• Flush the toilet • Put paper towels in trash • Turn off water & lights
Van/bus	• Buckle up • Face front • Use indoor voices	• Keep hands & feet to self • Listen to the bus driver	• Pick up your things
Clean up/ transitions	• Use walking feet • Use listening ears • Stay with your teacher	• Use inside voices • Leave space for others in line	• Help your friends • Put toys away • Follow the line • Hold the door

Figure A.2. Busy Bee Preschool behavior matrix using the three buzz words. (*Source:* Stormont, Lewis, & Beckner, 2005.)

recognition paired with a bee sticker to place on the classroom beehive (see classroom bulletin boards). Then, the class will earn a group reward or special activity, such as pajama parties, bubble-blowing parties, or silly hat days. This motivates the children to continue the appropriate behavior and to work toward achieving the class celebration. Slowly, the stickers become less frequent as the expected behaviors become an established part of the classroom culture.

A Consistent Approach for Responding to Challenging Behaviors

The positive behavior support team has developed a sequence for responding to children's challenging behaviors (see Figure A.3), including using the definitions from BIRS-NH (Muscott and Pomerleau, 2008) and developmentally appropriate consequences when deemed necessary (see the list of challenging behavior definitions below).

Challenging Behavior Definitions

1. *Physical aggression:* Forceful physical actions directed toward adults or peers that may result in physical contact and injury (e.g., hitting, kicking, spitting, pinching, and throwing objects)

2. *Self-injury:* Physical actions directed toward oneself, which may result in visible injury (e.g., hitting, kicking, scratching, pinching oneself)

3. *Disruption/tantrum:* An outburst or action that prevents learning or interferes with teaching and persists despite an adult's request to stop or attempt to provide support

4. *Inappropriate language:* The repeated use of words or phrases that are typically unexpected for the child's developmental age or level (e.g., swearing, profanity, sexual explicitness) despite the request of an adult to stop

5. *Verbal aggression:* The use of threatening, offensive, or intimidating words directed toward a peer or adult (e.g., screaming, name calling, swearing, profanity, threats)

6. *Noncompliance:* Refusal to follow a reasonable request, direction, or the established routine that persists after multiple requests and a reasonable amount of time

7. *Social withdrawal/isolation:* Nonparticipation in class activities or withdrawal from play or social interactions with peers or adults that interferes with the child's ability to learn and interact with others, which is outside the typical range of temperament

8. *Running away:* The act of leaving a designated area of supervision/boundary of play without permission and without responding to the requests of an adult to return

9. *Property damage:* Purposeful actions directed toward items or property that may have destructive results (e.g., ripping of books, knocking over shelves, throwing chairs)

10. *Unsafe behaviors:* Physical actions that may directly or indirectly result in physical injury to self or others that persist despite an adult's request to stop and are unexpected based on the developmental age and/or level of the child (e.g., climbing on furniture, running into people or things, inappropriate use of materials)

Busy Bee Positive Behavior Curriculum

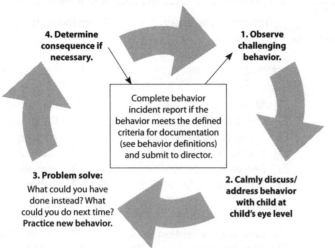

4. Determine consequence if necessary.

1. Observe challenging behavior.

Complete behavior incident report if the behavior meets the defined criteria for documentation (see behavior definitions) and submit to director.

3. Problem solve: What could you have done instead? What could you do next time? Practice new behavior.

2. Calmly discuss/ address behavior with child at child's eye level

Figure A.3. Sequence for responding to children's challenging behaviors. (From New Hampton Child Care Center; reprinted by permission.)

Data Need to Be Collected, Reviewed, and Used to Monitor Progress and Make Decisions Related to Program Improvement

When challenging behaviors in the classroom exceed developmental norms or are beyond what is expected misbehavior for the age and developmental level of the child, the incident will be tracked on a behavior incident report (BIR) and submitted to the director for entry into a data management program (see Figure A.4). This information will be collected and reviewed regularly by the positive behavior support team for the purpose of making informed decisions regarding what skills to teach children, what cool tools will be developed for program-wide skill development, and when group and/or individualized supports are needed for specific children. Parents will be contacted and communication will remain open and supportive if a child's behaviors become concerning to the staff of Busy Bee Preschool. Every effort will be made to partner with parents and find the supports that will most benefit the child.

These main ideas of the PW-PBIS program, implemented in all of our classrooms, will support children in their social-emotional development, keep our classrooms positive and consistent, and most importantly, establish a safe and responsive environment in which all children can learn, play, and grow.

Additional Supports

For some children, teaching and acknowledging appropriate behaviors may not be enough support. Some children may have a more difficult time adjusting to the classroom expectations and structure. The Busy Bee program will offer additional support for these children. The Busy Bee Preschool includes a positive behavior support team designed to target specific behaviors. The team will develop a plan to help minimize inappropriate behaviors and teach new skills for these children. The members are trained to observe children in the preschool setting and to determine individual needs for behavior support. With parent input, we will work together to either offer small group social skill instruction or to create an individual behavior support plan to meet the child's specific behavioral needs. Any parent is welcome to seek assistance from the Busy Bee positive behavior support team by contacting your child's teacher or the center director.

Behavior Incident Report

Child's name/code: _____ Program: _____ Classroom: _____

Date: _____ Time of occurrence: _____ Referring staff: _____

Severity: Mild   Moderate   Severe

ROUTINE (check one)

- ❏ Arrival
- ❏ Classroom jobs
- ❏ Circle/large group activity
- ❏ Small group activity
- ❏ Centers/workshops

- ❏ Meals
- ❏ Quiet time/nap
- ❏ Outdoor play
- ❏ Special activity/field trip
- ❏ Self-care/bathroom
- ❏ Transition

- ❏ Departure
- ❏ Clean-up
- ❏ Therapy
- ❏ Individual activity
- ❏ Free play
- ❏ Other _____

MOTIVATION (check up to 2)

- ❏ Obtain desired item
- ❏ Obtain desired activity
- ❏ Gain peer attention

- ❏ Gain adult attention
- ❏ Obtain sensory
- ❏ Avoid task/activity
- ❏ Avoid peers

- ❏ Avoid adults
- ❏ Avoid sensory
- ❏ Don't know
- ❏ Other _____

CHALLENGING BEHAVIOR (check up to 3)

- ❏ Physical aggression
- ❏ Self injury
- ❏ Disruption/Tantrum
- ❏ Inappropriate language

- ❏ Verbal aggression
- ❏ Noncompliance
- ❏ Social withdrawal/isolation

- ❏ Running away
- ❏ Property damage
- ❏ Unsafe behaviors
- ❏ Other _____

INVOLVED PERSONS (check all that apply)

- ❏ Assistant teacher
- ❏ Peers
- ❏ Other _____

- ❏ Teacher
- ❏ None
- ❏ Substitute

- ❏ Support/admin. staff
- ❏ Family member
- ❏ Therapist

TEACHER/STAFF RESPONSE (check the most intrusive)

- ❏ Re-Teach/practice
- ❏ Verbal reminder
- ❏ Remove from area
- ❏ Physical guidance

- ❏ Curriculum modification
- ❏ Family contact
- ❏ Loss of item/privilege
- ❏ Move within group

- ❏ Time with adult in different classroom/support staff
- ❏ Remove from activity
- ❏ Physical hold/Restrain
- ❏ Other _____

ADMINISTRATIVE FOLLOW-UP (check the most intrusive)

- ❏ Nonapplicable
- ❏ Talk with child
- ❏ Telephone contact with parent/family

- ❏ Parent/family meeting
- ❏ Reduce hours in program
- ❏ Arrange behavioral consultation/team

- ❏ Targeted group intervention
- ❏ Transfer to another program
- ❏ Dismissal
- ❏ Other _____

Comments: _____

_____

Figure A.4. Behavior incident report. (From New Hampshire Center for Effective Behavioral Interventions and Supports [2009]. *BIRS-NH Data Collection Form.* Bedford, NH: New Hampshire Center for Effective Behavioral Interventions and Supports; adapted by permission.)

Busy Bee Preschool Home Connection

What's the BUZZ at Busy Bee Preschool?

Dear Parent(s),

We at Busy Bee Preschool are interested in having you join us as we strive to teach your children appropriate behaviors. In this letter, you will find ways to get in on the latest buzz and reinforce what is being taught at preschool. We value partnering with you in your child's education!

This month, at Busy Bee Preschool, we will be focusing on the following:

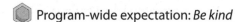 Program-wide expectation: *Be kind*

Specific skill being taught: *Take turns*

What Can You Do at Home?

First, talk about taking turns by saying the following:

"It's important to be kind to your friends by taking turns. It can be hard to take turns sometimes, but it is what kind friends do for each other. Taking turns helps everyone have fun when you are playing a game, and if everyone has fun, then your friends will want to play more games with you."

Next, practice! Try the following:

Play a fun family game or with toys that require turn taking, such as Candy Land, Connect Four, or Go Fish, or take turns throwing a ball into a laundry basket or placing blocks on a tower. Use cues such as "my turn" and "your turn" if your child has difficulty knowing when to take turns. Involve the whole family and keep it fun!

Then, reinforce and acknowledge your child for using this new skill by stating the following:

"Oh, I'm so proud of you; you waited to take your turn!"
"Thank you for letting me have a turn! That was so kind!" Be sure to offer high fives, smiles, hugs, and kisses for being kind and taking turns!

Thanks for your help in partnering with us to teach your child
the latest BUZZ at Busy Bee Preschool!

Our Busy Bee buzz words

BE SAFE

BE KIND

BE HELPFUL

The Curriculum and Families

All of these strategies can be used in the home as well as at Busy Bee Preschool. In fact, the program's effectiveness increases when more people in a child's life are using the same strategies. For example, if both the preschool and family are using words like *be safe, be kind,* and *be helpful* when discussing behavior, the message to the child that these are important and valued behaviors becomes stronger.

Be sure to talk to your child about the skills he or she is learning at preschool. Help your child practice these behaviors at home and provide reminders of the Busy Bee buzz words (be safe, be kind, be helpful) as you drive to school in the morning or any other time during the day. Let your child know that his or her behavior at school is important to you. Let your child know that you are proud of how well he or she is learning to get along with others, follow directions, share, work, and play together. Be sure to read our monthly Busy Bee Preschool Home Connection (see included sample) for ideas on how to encourage these important skills at home. Parents can also hang a copy of the expectations in the home as a reminder that these expectations are important all the time, not only in preschool.

Positive Parenting

Another way that this same strategy can be useful for families is by helping parents deal with challenging behaviors in the home. Parenting is one of the hardest jobs, and doing it well is more important than any other job. Helping children learn appropriate behavior will help them to be more successful in every part of their lives, from preschool through adulthood. Using the same basic concepts, we have come up with three buzz words for positive parenting in order to help carry these strategies into the home:

 BE POSITIVE

 BE FIRM

 BE CONSISTENT

Using these three buzz words as parenting guidelines will help you to encourage the development of positive behaviors in your child. Some examples of these strategies put into practice include the following:

1. Praise your child when he or she is behaving appropriately. Make an effort to notice your child being good more often and reward that behavior. The reward does not have to be a prize but can be praise or special time with you such as reading a book, taking a walk, or coloring with you.

2. Try to say at least four positive statements for each negative or corrective statement you say to your child. Something as quick as "nice job" or "you are such a good helper" can have a huge effect on your child's self-esteem.

3. Separate how you feel about a child from how you feel about the child's behavior. Instead of saying "you are a bad boy," you can say, "I don't like it when you hit" or, even better, "We need to keep our hands to ourselves."

4. Give your child examples of what to do and not to do. For example, instead of saying, "No, don't put that in your mouth," you can say, "Toys are for playing with. If you are hungry, eat a snack."

5. State the rules calmly. Be firm and neutral in your tone of voice. Children often misbehave to get attention. Even negative attention, such as yelling, can be a reward for the child and will reinforce the inappropriate behavior. Tell the child what behavior you want to see and stay calm.

6. Stay firm in your decisions. Once you have told the child your expectations, do not change your mind because a child whines, yells, or cries. Doing this will teach your child that the behavior works and your child will repeat the behavior again and again. This is often the hardest thing for parents to do, but staying firm will help both you and your child prevent more intense behavior later.

7. Be consistent in your expectations and your reactions to inappropriate behavior. If you have a rule that there is no jumping on the bed, then every time your child does that you must redirect and remind him or her that it is not safe. Having the same consequence each time will let your child know that you mean what you say, which will prevent it from recurring.

8. Being consistent in your family's daily routines can also help your child's behavior. Routines help children feel safe by letting them know what to expect from their surroundings. This is especially true with morning, mealtime, and bedtime routines. Do things in the same order each day. As an example, each night the child may take a bath followed by a snack, brushing teeth, a story, and then bed. Keeping this as consistent as possible will help your child know the expectations and follow the routine.

9. Be a good role model. Children notice everything that the adults in their world do. If children see adults being safe, kind, and helpful in their own lives, then it teaches children to do the same. If you treat children with respect and care, they will grow to be respectful and caring adults. If you are positive with children, they will look at their world as a safe and positive place and have positive and healthy relationships with the other people in their world.

10. Finally, slow down. Often, the pace of the adult world is overwhelming for young children. Take time to smell the flowers—even we at Busy Bee can learn to make time for that!

This program can help everyone in children's lives to be more effective in dealing with behaviors. Helping children learn the skills they need to get along with others is very important. If you have any questions, please feel free to talk to your child's teacher or the director. Together, we can give all our Busy Bee children a positive, successful start!

PRACTICE ADMINISTERING THE PreSET AT BUSY BEE PRESCHOOL

Now that you are familiar with Busy Bee Preschool, use the following partially completed PreSET scoring materials to give Busy Bee a PreSET score:

- The sample PreSET Administrator Interview Form (see Figure A.5), which has been filled out as if you had interviewed Busy Bee's administrator yourself

- The partially completed PreSET Classroom Interview and Observation Form for Classroom 1 (see Figure A.6)

- The partially completed PreSET Classroom Interview and Observation Form for Classroom 2 (see Figure A.7)

- The partially completed PreSET Classroom Interview and Observation Form for Classroom 3 (see Figure A.8)

Use the information provided in Figure A.5 and the partial information provided in Figures A.6–A.8 to fill in the scores on Figures A.6–A.8. Then transfer your scores to the blank PreSET Classroom Summary Form and the blank PreSET Scoring Guide in Figures A.9 and A.10, respectively. When you are finished, check your work against the following answer keys:

- The fully completed PreSET Classroom Interview and Observation Form for Classroom 1 (see Figure A.11)

- The fully completed PreSET Classroom Interview and Observation Form for Classroom 2 (see Figure A.12)

- The fully completed PreSET Classroom Interview and Observation Form for Classroom 3 (see Figure A.13)

- The completed PreSET Classroom Summary Form (see Figure A.14)

- The completed PreSET Scoring Guide (see Figure A.15)

PreSET. Administrator Interview Form

I. General information

Program/preschool name: _Busy Bee Preschool_ Date of interview: _9/15/10_

Program contact information (telephone/e-mail): _444-1234; busybeepreschool@internet.com_

Administrator interviewed: _C. Smith_

II. Products to collect

In order to maximize efficiency, it is recommended that the evaluator request that the following items be prepared ahead of time. The materials will then be readily available on the day of the scheduled Preschool-Wide Evaluation Tool™ (PreSET™) visit. If this is not possible, inquire if someone would be able to gather the products while the PreSET is being conducted. It is important to note that many preschool classrooms may not have developed the listed materials yet. Every attempt should be made to assure administrators and/or classroom teachers that they are not expected to have all of these materials, especially if the PreSET is being conducted prior to program-wide positive behavior intervention and support (PW-PBIS) implementation.

a. Program handbook

b. Behavior expectations/matrix

c. Lesson plan(s) or cool tool(s) documenting the teaching of the classroom expectations *for each classroom* implementing PW-PBIS (ideally seeking evidence that the classroom rules were directly taught to the children more than once in each classroom)

d. Acknowledgment/reinforcement plan

e. Behavior incident flow chart

f. Behavior incident report (BIR) form or another data collection form that documents children's challenging behavior daily

g. PW-PBIS action plan

h. Written communication to families regarding PW-PBIS strategies in the classroom (e.g., newsletters, memos, announcements)

Figure A.5. Sample completed PreSET Administrator Interview Form for the Busy Bee Preschool case study.

(continued)

PreSET

"Let's start by discussing general information about the program…"

III. Data on program

1. Type of program (circle all that apply):

   a. Head Start   d. Corporate sponsored   g. District   j. Preschool in elementary school

   b. Early Head Start   (e.) Franchise   h. State-funded pre-K   k. Other _____

   c. Private   f. Nonprofit   i. Special education classroom

2. Hours of operation (circle appropriate choices):

   a. Part day   (b.) Full day   c. Extended day (before/after care)

3. Length of service year (circle appropriate choices):

   a. 9 or 10 months (school year)   (b.) 12 months (full year)   c. Other (Please specify) _____

4. Does the program include children with disabilities (e.g., children who have an individualized education program [IEP] or individualized family service plan [IFSP])?

   (a.) Yes   b. No

5. Does the program include children for whom English is a second language?

   (a.) Yes   b. No   *Note, if yes, please write the language(s) children speak at home:*   Spanish

6. Does the program receive state subsidies (e.g., child care subsidies)?

   (a.) Yes   b. No

Notes: *Possible things to discuss include the curricular approach, mission, and any unique characteristics of the children and families that attend the program.*

The Busy Bee Preschool program has been operating for 12 years and uses the HighScope curriculum for planning instruction during regular classroom routines. We use the plan-do-review sequence with children as part of this curriculum in our three preschool classrooms. We have one 3's classroom, 1 multiage classroom (3–5), and one prekindergarten classroom (4–5). In the last 2 years, we've been part of the state-wide initiative to implement positive behavior support. Children and families come from the surrounding working and lower middle class neighborhoods. The families are very involved, although their involvement varies. We have quite a few dual-income families that find it hard to participate in the classroom as much as they'd like.

"I would like to gather some information about the individual classrooms as well..."

IV. Data on individual classrooms (to be collected through interviews with the program director and/or classroom teachers)

Prompt to evaluator: Fill in the names or numbers of the classrooms in the left-hand column below. Decide whether the data in the section are best collected at this facility through the administrator interview or individual classroom interviews.

Classroom name/ number	Ages served	Number of children	Number of children with an IFSP/IEP	Number of children expelled		Number of staff regularly sched-uled to work in classroom	Number of staff at each credential level (HS, CDA, AA, BA/BS, PB)	Number of staff who left program	Number of newly hired staff
				No IEP	IEP				
1. Preschool 1	3–4	16	2	0	0	2	AA: 1 HS: 1	0	0
2. Preschool 2	3–5	18	1	0	0	2	BA/BS: 1 CDA: 1	1	1
3. Preschool 3	4–5	24	4	1	0	3	AA: 2 HS: 1	2	3
4.									
5.									
6.									
7.									
8.									
9.									
10.									
Totals for program		58	7	1	0	7		3	4

Key: AA, associate of arts; BA/BS, bachelor of arts/bachelor of science; CDA, child development associate;   HS, high school; PB, postbaccalaureate.

(continued)

"Let's talk about the program, starting with the behavioral expectations that you have established ..."

V. Behavioral Expectations Defined and Taught (Features A and B)

A1	Has the program agreed to five or fewer positively stated expectations that are posted and the same for each classroom? *(Note: If the answer is "no" to A1, you may skip to "VI. Responses to Appropriate and Challenging Behavior" [Feature C].)*	No	Yes, but more than five, negatively stated, and/or classrooms have their own expectations	Yes
Use answer to corroborate teachers' responses during classroom interview **(B2)**	(If the program has rules) What are the rules?	*Be safe* *Be kind* *Be helpful*		
Use answer to corroborate teachers' responses during classroom interview **(B1)**	(If the program has rules) How are the program's rules taught in each classroom?	*Daily review during circle time, children sing rules song along with our mascot the bee puppet each day, practice one key rule that they're working on during circle through discussion, modeling, or role play*		

Notes: *Behavioral Expectations Defined and Taught (Features A and B):*

"Now I'd like to ask you about how the children know that they are meeting expectations…"

VI. Responses to Appropriate and Challenging Behavior (Feature C)

	No	Yes, (implemented once a day)	Yes, implemented more than once a day
C1 Is there a system for acknowledging children's appropriate behavior that is frequently used in each classroom (e.g., special spotlight or raffle during circle, tokens for children who clean up after discovery)? (If yes) How often is it implemented? *(Note: If the answer is "no" to C1, you may skip to C3.)*			
Use answer to corroborate teachers' responses during classroom interview **(C2)** (If the program has a system) Please describe. *Children earn Bee stickers to place on the class Beehive poster, when the beehive is full, they celebrate with a "Busy Bee" class party*			
(If the program has a system) Do you perceive that it is implemented consistently across teachers? *(Note: Consistency of implementation is measured by observation of teachers in their classrooms; this is just additional information.)*	No		(Yes)

"Now I'd like to ask you about how children's challenging behavior is handled…"

	No	Yes, but procedure is basic (e.g., redirection is the only response identified)	Yes
C3 Does the program have a procedure for responding to children's challenging behavior that is hierarchical and function based (e.g., restate classroom rule, redirection to another activity, reteach skill, removal from area)? *(Note: If the answer is "no" to C3, you may skip to "VII Monitoring and Decision Making" [Feature E].)*			(Yes)
Use answer to corroborate teachers' responses during classroom interview **(C4)** (If the program has a procedure) Please describe or attach program's behavior flow chart to interview form. *Stop. Talk about the issue or redirect if possible. Problem solve and practice a new way to handle the problem, determine consequence if it is necessary. If the behavior meets the definition of "trackable" behaviors, the teacher completes a behavior incident report and submits it to me.*			
(If the program has a procedure) Do you perceive that it is implemented consistently across teachers? *(Note: Consistency of implementation is measured by observation of teachers in their classrooms; this is just additional information.)*	(No)		Yes

Notes: *Responses to Appropriate and Challenging Behavior (Feature C):* The teachers all implement the Beehive acknowledgment system "for the most part." They "are still working on that part" (referring to consistency of system to respond to challenging behavior).

(continued)

71

PreSET

"I'd like to briefly discuss how incidents of challenging behavior are documented…"

VII. Monitoring and Decision Making (Feature E)

		No	Yes, but not used daily or is only anecdotal	Yes
E1	Is there a data collection form that is used daily to document children's challenging behavior? *(Note: If the answer is "no" to E1, you may skip to "VIII. Family Involvement" [Feature F].)*			(Yes)
Use answer to corroborate teachers' responses during classroom interview **(E2)**	(If the program has a data collection form) Please describe and attach form to interview form.			*The teachers document challenging behaviors on the behavior incident report. We track information about the behavior, the time of the incident, the date, the people involved, the routine in which it occurred, the possible motivation, the teacher response, and sometimes the administrator response if I need to get involved. I enter that information into a web-based data system to track the information. Note: Form included in Parent Handbook.*
E3: Part I	(If the program has a data collection form) Is a software system (e.g., Excel, web-based system) used to enter and summarize data collected about children's challenging behavior?	No		(Yes)
E3: Part II	(If the program has a software system) What software do you use for entering and summarizing information about children's challenging behavior?			*The Behavior Incident Reporting System–New Hampshire (BIRS-NH)*

		No system or data not entered	Less than monthly	At least monthly
E3: Part III	(If the program has a software system) How often are behavior incident data entered into the system?			(At least monthly)
E3: Part IV	(If the program has a software system) Who inputs and summarizes the data?	*Program administrator*		
E4	(If the program has a software system or data collection form) How often are the data reviewed for decision making?	No system or data not reviewed	(Less than monthly)	At least monthly

Notes: *Monitoring and Decision Making (Feature E):*

I try to review the data on BIRS-NH prior to each team meeting, but it probably averages out to be every other month or so that I actually review the data.

PreSET

(Note: If the answer to A1 was "no" and the program does not have established rules, you need only ask questions related to F5 in the following section.)

"Next, let's talk about how families are involved in the program's effort to support children's behavior..."

VIII. Family Involvement (Feature F)

F3	(If the program has expectations) Were families included in the development and/or revision of program expectations? *(Note: Families don't need to be asked or involved each year, just at some point in their development.)*	No expectations or families not included		Yes
F4	(If the program has expectations) Are families notified of program expectations in writing at least annually?	No expectations or families not notified	Yes, but not in writing	Yes
F5	Are families notified of PW-PBIS strategies (e.g., how teachers teach social skills or respond to challenging behavior) in writing at least annually? *(Note: Please verify with products such as the program handbook.)*	No	Yes, but not in writing	Yes

Notes: *Family Involvement (Feature F):*

"The next questions are about whether there is an established team of professionals to meet regularly regarding children's social-emotional development and the prevention of challenging behavior in the classroom..."

IX. Management (Feature G)

G1	Is there an established team to address PW-PBIS (e.g., teaching and acknowledging behavioral expectations, developing a system for responding to challenging behavior)? *(Note: If the answer is "no" to G1, you may skip to "X. Program Support" [Feature H].)*		No	Yes
G3	(If there is a team) List each position/role represented (e.g., teacher, assistant teacher, administrator, specialist, family member).	Myself – Director 2 Lead Preschool Teachers Behavior Consultant 1 Parent that comes every other month 1 Assistant Teacher		

(continued)

PreSET

IX. Management (Feature G) *(continued)*

		No team or no meeting	Less than monthly	At least monthly
G4	(If there is a team) How often does the team meet?			(At least monthly)
		No or less than once a year, or no team	Yes, but only once a year	Yes, at least twice a year
G5	(If there is a team) Does the team report progress related to PW-PBIS goals to all program staff at least twice a year?			(Yes, at least twice a year)
		No team or no action plan	Yes, but it's over a year old	Yes, current plan
G6	(If there is a team) Does the team have an action plan for implementing PW-PBIS that is less than one year old? *(Note: Please review the actual action plan.)*	(No team or no action plan)		

Notes: *Management (Feature G):*

"The last questions relate to positive behavior support efforts that are supported with funding, planning time, and professional development..."

X. Program Support (Feature H)

		No	Budget established, but insufficient funds	Yes
H1	Does the program have a budget with sufficient funds for building and maintaining PW-PBIS (e.g., materials, training for teachers, conference attendance)?			(Yes)
		No	Yes, but limited planning time or resources	Yes
H2	Are teachers provided with the time and resources (e.g., time to plan teaching lessons, money for rules posters) needed to implement goals related to PW-PBIS?		(Yes, but limited planning time or resources)	
		No	Yes, but it was over a year ago	Yes, in the last academic year
H3	Has there been at least one professional development opportunity for staff related to PW-PBIS? (If yes) When did the last one occur?			(Yes, in the last academic year)

Notes: *Program Support (Feature H):* It's hard to give teachers time for planning; they do that on their own. They always can get the supplies they need though.

PreSET™ Classroom Interview and Observation Form

Program: _Busy Bee Preschool_ Classroom: _Preschool 1_ Date: _9/15/10_

Use the information you have learned about **Busy Bee Preschool** in the preceding case study to give them a PreSET score.

Teacher Questions

Interview up to three teachers

Respondent:	What are the program's rules? (B2) Record number known that match program's rules. (Note: Automatically circle "no" if no program rules established.)		What happens after (circle time)? (D2) Must agree with posted classroom schedule and each other.
	Number Known	Number of Rules	Record + or –
Teacher 1	3	3	+
Teacher 2	2	3	+
Teacher 3			
Scoring	Did all interviewed teachers state the majority of the program rules? Yes No		Did all interviewed teachers correctly state what happens after (circle time)? Yes No

Children's Questions

A teacher should ask three children the following two questions. Use verbal prompting and accommodations for children's language abilities as necessary.

Respondent:	What are the rules in your classroom? (B3) Record number known that match program's rules. (Note: Automatically circle "no" if no program rules established.)		What happens after (circle time)? (D3) Must agree with posted classroom schedule and teachers.
	Number Known	Number of Rules	Record + or –
Child 1	3	3	+
Child 2	3	3	+
Child 3	3	3	+
Scoring	Did all interviewed children state the majority of the classroom rules? Yes No		Did all interviewed children correctly state what happens after (circle time)? Yes No

Lead Teacher Questions

How do you teach the program rules in your classroom? (B1) (Note: Automatically circle "no" if no program rules established.)	How do you acknowledge appropriate behavior? (C2) (Note: Automatically circle "no" if no system identified by administrator.)	How do you respond to challenging behavior? (C4) (Note: Automatically circle "no" if no procedure identified by administrator.)	What do you use to collect data on children's challenging behavior? (E2) (Note: Automatically circle "no" if no data form identified by administrator.)	How do you communicate with families? (F1)	How do families participate in the classroom? (F2)	(If there is a PBS team) What is the function of the program's PBS team? (G2) (Note: Automatically circle "no" if no program-wide PBS team established.)	Do you have sufficient time for planning and enough resources to meet your teaching goals? (H4)
Review and sing rules during circle time using a Bee puppet; focus on the key Buzz word each month.	The children can earn bee stickers to add to the hive on the bulletin board.	Either redirect or talk about the issue, problem solve, and practice a new solution; some behaviors are tracked on a form.	Behavior incident form.	Daily at drop off and pick up, monthly newsletters, e-mail, parent conferences 2x per year, phone calls as needed.	Some parents will come in and have lunch with their children; field trip volunteers, provide requested supplies, read a story to the children.	They create, change, and add to the program's Behavior Curriculum to keep consistency in each classroom, determine skills to focus on monthly for teaching rules.	Somewhat. I wish I had more planning time. I get supplies I need.
Program rules are taught in large or small groups? Yes* No *Must see a lesson plan to score "yes."	Is there a system? Yes* No *The system must match the program's, and you must observe its use or evidence of its use to score "yes."	Is there a procedure? Yes* No *The procedure must match the program's, and you must observe its use or evidence of its use to score "yes."	Data collection form? Yes* No *The form must match the program's, form and you must observe its use or evidence of its use to score "yes."	Communicate with families? Yes* No *Must include at least one other way besides pick up and drop off to score "yes" (e.g., e-mail, phone, home visits).	Families participate in the classroom (e.g., classroom helpers, readers)? Yes No	(If there is a PBS team) Correct function of the PW-PBS team? Yes No	Sufficient planning time and adequate resources? Yes No

Figure A.6. Partially completed PreSET Classroom Interview and Observation Form for Classroom 1.

(continued)

Figure A.6. *(continued)*

PreSET

Classroom Environment

Use the items in italics to score the presence or absence of the following items in the classroom. *(Note: Automatically circle "no" for A2, A3, and A4 if no program rules established.)*

Are program rules posted in at least one classroom location at eye level? *Wall poster(s) (A2)*	Do program rules include a combination of words and visuals? *Wall poster(s) (A3)*	Are program rules incorporated into a matrix of expectations for classroom routines? *Matrix of classroom rules (A4)*	Is there a posted classroom schedule that includes visual pictures at eye level for children on at least one wall? *Classroom schedule (D1)*
(Yes) No	(Yes) No	Yes No	Yes (No)

10-minute Classroom Observation

Observe during a classroom routine such as free play, circle time, or snack; choose one teacher to observe.
Time started: 9:05   Time ended: 9:15

Tally the number of positive statements (praise, approval) (C5)	Tally the number of negative statements (reprimand, correction, disapproval) (C5)	Tally the number of comments using specific verbal praise (C6)
////	/	///

Divide the number of positive statements by the number of negative statements:

_____ / _____ = _____

Is the result a number of 4.0 or greater?
Yes   No

Transition

Observe at least one transition from an unstructured or less structured activity (e.g., free play, outside) to a more structured activity (e.g., circle time, snack time).

Did at least one teacher use a precorrection (e.g., remind a child of a classroom rule in the absence of misbehavior) at least once? (C7)	Did at least one teacher use a system other than or in addition to a verbal direction to signal the transition (e.g., ring bell, hand motion, sing song)? (D4)	Did at least one teacher provide a notice before the transition signal (e.g., play time over in 2 minutes)? (D5)
Yes (No)	Yes (No)	Yes (No)

Was there at least 1?
Yes   No

*Use the information you have learned about **Busy Bee Preschool** in the preceding case study to give them a PreSET score.*

Notes:
Classroom schedule posted with pictures but not at eye level for children.

PreSET · Classroom Interview and Observation Form

Program: _Busy Bee Preschool_ Classroom: _Preschool 2_ Date: _9/15/10_

Teacher Questions
Interview up to three teachers

Respondent:	What are the program's rules? (B2) Record number known that match program's rules (Note: Automatically circle "no" if no program rules established.)		What happens after (circle time)? (D2) Must agree with posted classroom schedule and each other. Record + or –
	Number Known	Number of Rules	Record + or –
Teacher 1	3	3	+
Teacher 2	2	3	–
Teacher 3			
Scoring	Did all interviewed teachers state the majority of the program rules? Yes No		Did all interviewed teachers correctly state what happens after (circle time)? Yes No

Children's Questions
A teacher should ask three children the following two questions. Use verbal prompting and accommodations for children's language abilities as necessary.

Respondent:	What are the rules in your classroom? (B3) Record number known that match program's rules (Note: Automatically circle "no" if no program rules established.)		What happens after (circle time)? (D3) Must agree with posted classroom schedule and teachers. Record + or –
	Number Known	Number of Rules	Record + or –
Child 1	3	3	+
Child 2	2	3	–
Child 3	2	3	–
Scoring	Did all interviewed children state the majority of the classroom rules? Yes No		Did all interviewed children correctly state what happens after (circle time)? Yes No

> Use the information you have learned about **Busy Bee Preschool** in the preceding case study to give them a PreSET score.

Lead Teacher Questions

How do you teach the program rules in your classroom? (B1) (Note: Automatically circle "no" if no program rules established.)	How do you acknowledge appropriate behavior? (C2) (Note: Automatically circle "no" if no system identified by administrator.)	How do you respond to challenging behavior? (C4) (Note: Automatically circle "no" if no procedure identified by administrator.)	What do you use to collect data on children's challenging behavior? (E2) (Note: Automatically circle "no" if no data form identified by administrator.)
Sing rules every day at circle time with puppets.	I give the children Bee stickers for the class Beehive; then when the Hive is full, we have a class party.	Try to redirect whenever possible, then talk with the child at his or her level, practice a new skill for next time it occurs, sometimes document if needed.	Behavior incident form.
Program rules are taught in large or small groups? Yes* No *Must see a lesson plan to score "yes"	Is there a system? Yes* No *The system must match the program's and you must observe its use or evidence of its use to score "yes"	Is there a procedure? Yes* No *The procedure must match the program's and you must observe its use or evidence of its use to score "yes"	Data collection form? Yes* No *The form must match the program's form and you must observe its use or evidence of its use to score "yes"

How do you communicate with families? (F1)	How do families participate in the classroom? (F2)	(If there is a PBS team) What is the function of the program's PBS team? (G2) (Note: Automatically circle "no" if no program-wide PBS team established.)	Do you have sufficient time for planning and enough resources to meet your teaching goals? (H4)
Each day when they drop off and pick up their child, sometimes phone calls, e-mail, monthly newsletter.	They volunteer for field trips, help with class supplies—most are working so we don't see them a lot in the classroom. The same ones volunteer all of the time.	They come up with skills for us to focus on during circle and review our behavior data; they work on improving the data system and getting us to consistently use it.	Sort of. We never get time to lesson plan but I usually always get what I want for materials and I get reimbursed if I get it on my own.
Communicate with families? Yes* No *Must include at least one other way besides pick up and drop off to score "yes" (e.g., e-mail, phone, home visits)	Families participate in the classroom (e.g., classroom helpers, readers)? Yes No	(If there is a PBS team) Correct function of the PW-PBS team? Yes No	Sufficient planning time and adequate resources? Yes No

Figure A.7. Partially completed PreSET Classroom Interview and Observation Form for Classroom 2.

(continued)

Figure A.7. *(continued)*

⊛ PreSET

Classroom Environment

Use the items in italics to score the presence or absence of the following items in the classroom. *(Note: Automatically circle "no" for A2, A3, and A4 if no program rules established.)*

Are program rules posted in at least one classroom location at eye level? *Wall poster(s) (A2)*	Do program rules include a combination of words and visuals? *Wall poster(s) (A3)*	Are program rules incorporated into a matrix of expectations for classroom routines? *Matrix of classroom rules (A4)*	Is there a posted classroom schedule that includes visual pictures at eye level for children on at least one wall? *Classroom schedule (D1)*
(Yes) No	(Yes) No	(Yes) No	Yes (No)

10-minute Classroom Observation

Observe during a classroom routine such as free play, circle time, or snack; choose one teacher to observe.
Time started: 9:35____   Time ended: 9:45____

Tally the number of positive statements (praise, approval) (C5)	Tally the number of negative statements (reprimand, correction, disapproval) (C5)	Tally the number of comments using specific verbal praise (C6)
///	//	/

Divide the number of positive statements by the number of negative statements:

____ / ____ = ____

Is the result a number of 4.0 or greater?   Yes   No

Was there at least 1?   Yes   No

Transition

Observe at least one transition from an unstructured or less structured activity (e.g., free play, outside) to a more structured activity (e.g., circle time, snack time).

Did at least one teacher use a pre-correction (e.g., remind a child of a classroom rule in the absence of misbehavior) at least once? (C7)	Did at least one teacher use a system other than or in addition to a verbal direction to signal the transition (e.g., ring bell, hand motion, sing song)? (D4)	Did at least one teacher provide a notice before the transition signal (e.g., play time over in 2 minutes)? (D5)
Yes (No)	Yes (No)	Yes (No)

*Use the information you have learned about **Busy Bee Preschool** in the preceding case study to give them a PreSET score.*

Notes:

Classroom schedule does not have pictures.

Assistant teacher has been working in this classroom for 8 weeks.

PreSET Classroom Interview and Observation Form

Program: Busy Bee Preschool   Classroom: Preschool 3   Date: 9/15/10

Teacher Questions
Interview up to three teachers

Respondent:	What are the program's rules? (B2) Record number known that match program's rules (Note: Automatically circle "no" if no program rules established.)		What happens after (circle time)? (D2) Must agree with posted classroom schedule and each other. Record + or –
	Number Known	Number of Rules	
Teacher 1	2	3	– (no schedule posted)
Teacher 2	1	3	–
Teacher 3	0	3	–
Scoring	Did all interviewed teachers state the majority of the program rules? Yes No		Did all interviewed teachers correctly state what happens after (circle time)? Yes No

Children's Questions
A teacher should ask three children the following two questions. Use verbal prompting and accommodations for children's language abilities as necessary.

Respondent:	What are the rules in your classroom? (B3) Record number known that match program's rules (Note: Automatically circle "no" if no program rules established.)		What happens after (circle time)? (D3) Must agree with posted classroom schedule and teachers. Record + or –
	Number Known	Number of Rules	
Child 1	1	3	–
Child 2	0	3	–
Child 3	1	3	–
Scoring	Did all interviewed children state the majority of the classroom rules? Yes No		Did all interviewed children correctly state what happens after (circle time)? Yes No

> Use the information you have learned about **Busy Bee Preschool** in the preceding case study to give them a PreSET score.

Lead Teacher Questions

Question	Response	Scoring
How do you teach the program rules in your classroom? (B1) (Note: Automatically circle "no" if no program rules established.)	I go over the rules poster at circle time everyday (pointed to the rules poster) – 5 rules that do not match program rules.	Program rules are taught in large or small groups? Yes* No *Must see a lesson plan to score "yes"
How do you acknowledge appropriate behavior? (C2) (Note: Automatically circle "no" if no system identified by administrator.)	I give lots of praise and high fives. We have Bee stickers for the Hive, but I don't use that. I use it sometimes for GREAT behavior only.	Is there a system? Yes* No *The system must match the program's and you must observe its use or evidence of its use to score "yes"
How do you respond to challenging behavior? (C4) (Note: Automatically circle "no" if no procedure identified by administrator.)	I usually just use the time-out strategy for most issues. Sometimes I remove an item or take away an activity.	Is there a procedure? Yes* No *The procedure must match the program's and you must observe its use or evidence of its use to score "yes"
What do you use to collect data on children's challenging behavior? (E2) (Note: Automatically circle "no" if no data form identified by administrator.)	I keep notes in a notebook for major incidents and share it with parents when they pick up their child.	Data collection form? Yes* No *The form must match the program's form and you must observe its use or evidence of its use to score "yes"
How do you communicate with families? (F1)	When they drop off and pick up their child. I spend more time talking to them at pick up probably.	Communicate with families? Yes* No *Must include at least one other way besides pick up and drop off to score "yes" (e.g., e-mail, phone, home visits)
How do families participate in the classroom? (F2)	These families work so they don't come into the classroom.	Families participate in the classroom (e.g., classroom helpers, readers)? Yes No
(If there is a PBS team) What is the function of the program's PBS team? (G2) (Note: Automatically circle "no" if no program-wide PBS team established.)	I think there's a team that meets, but I don't know what they do.	(If there is a PBS team) Correct function of the PW-PBS team? Yes No
Do you have sufficient time for planning and enough resources to meet your teaching goals? (H4)	I never have time to plan lessons or activities. I do that at home.	Sufficient planning time and adequate resources? Yes No

Figure A.8. Partially completed PreSET Classroom Interview and Observation Form for Classroom 3.

(continued)

Figure A.8. *(continued)*

PreSET

Classroom Environment

Use the items in italics to score the presence or absence of the following items in the classroom. *(Note: Automatically circle "no" for A2, A3, and A4 if no program rules established.)*

Are program rules posted in at least one classroom location at eye level? *Wall poster(s) (A2)*	Do program rules include a combination of words and visuals? *Wall poster(s) (A3)*	Are program rules incorporated into a matrix of expectations for classroom routines? *Matrix of classroom rules (A4)*	Is there a posted classroom schedule that includes visual pictures at eye level for children on at least one wall? *Classroom schedule (D1)*
Yes (No)	Yes (No)	(Yes) No	Yes (No)

10-minute Classroom Observation

Observe during a classroom routine such as free play, circle time, or snack; choose one teacher to observe.
Time started: 9:55   Time ended: 10:05

Tally the number of positive statements (praise, approval) (C5)	Tally the number of negative statements (reprimand, correction, disapproval) (C5)	Tally the number of comments using specific verbal praise (C6)
II	III	I

Divide the number of positive statements by the number of negative statements:

_____ =

Is the result a number of 4.0 or greater?
Yes   No

Transition

Observe at least one transition from an unstructured or less structured activity (e.g., free play, outside) to a more structured activity (e.g., circle time, snack time).

Did at least one teacher use precorrection (e.g., remind a child of a classroom rule in the absence of misbehavior) at least once? (C7)	Did at least one teacher use a system other than or in addition to a verbal direction to signal the transition (e.g., ring bell, hand motion, sing song)? (D4)	Did at least one teacher provide a notice before the transition signal (e.g., play time over in 2 minutes)? (D5)
Was there at least 1? Yes No	Yes (No)	(Yes) No

*Use the information you have learned about **Busy Bee Preschool** in the preceding case study to give them a PreSET score.*

Notes:

All new teachers. Lead teacher has been there 3 months. Assistant teacher 1 has been there 2 months. Assistant teacher 2 was a new position added to the program 3 weeks ago due to parent complaints regarding behavioral concerns in the classroom.

PreSET.

Classroom Summary Form

Instructions: For a given program, transfer each classroom's scores from the Classroom Interview and Observation Form. Note the score as Y (yes) or N (no). When all participating classrooms' scores are transferred, complete the summary indicating a 0, 1, or 2 score.

Classrooms:	Teachers state rules (B2)	Teachers state what happens next (D2)	Children state rules (B3)	Children state what happens next (D3)	Plan to teach classroom rules (B1)	System to acknowledge appropriate behavior (C2)	System for responding to challenging behavior (C4)	Data collection form (E2)	Communicate with families in at least one way *in addition to* drop off/pick up (F1)	Families participate in classroom (F2)	Correct function of PW-PBIS team (G2)	Sufficient time and access to resources (H4)	Rules posted at eye level (A2)	Rules include words and visuals (A3)	Matrix of classroom rules (A4)	Schedule with visual pictures at eye level (D1)	Ratio of 4:1 positive to negative statements (C5)	Specific verbal praise (C6)	Precorrection during transition (C7)	Transition signal (D4)	Notice before transition signal (D5)
	B2	D2	B3	D3	B1	C2	C4	E2	F1	F2	G2	H4	A2	A3	A4	D1	C5	C6	C7	D4	D5
Classroom 1																					
Classroom 2																					
Classroom 3																					
Classroom 4																					
Classroom 5																					
Classroom 6																					
Classroom 7																					
Classroom 8																					
Classroom 9																					
Classroom 10																					
Summary: (0 = No in all; 1 = Yes in half or less than half; 2 = Yes in majority)																					

Figure A.9. Blank PreSET Classroom Summary Form.

 **Scoring Guide**

Instructions: Transfer information obtained from the PreSET Administrator Interview Form and PreSET Classroom Summary Form to this scoring guide to determine the program's PreSET total score and percent implemented by feature. Each item on this scoring guide should be scored with a *0, 1,* or *2* according to the guidelines outlined in the evaluation question description.

Please see the PreSET Administrator Interview Form and PreSET Classroom Interview and Observation Form for directions on how to conduct interviews and observations with the program administrator, staff, and children.

Program: _____   Date: _____

Administrator: _____   Date of last PreSET and score: _____

City, State: _____   Number of classrooms: _____

PreSET data collector(s): _____

Notes: _____

_____

Feature	Evaluation question	Data source	Score (0, 1, 2)
A. Expectations Defined	1. Has the program agreed to five or fewer positively stated expectations? (*0* = no; *1* = yes, but more than five, negatively stated, and/or classrooms have their own expectations; *2* = yes)	Administrator Interview Form	
	2. Are the agreed-on rules publicly posted at children's eye level in classrooms? (*0* = no rules established or no; *1* = half or less than half; *2* = majority of classrooms)	Classroom Summary Form	
	3. Are the agreed-on rules posted with a combination of words and visuals in classrooms? (*0* = no rules established or no; *1* = half or less than half; *2* = majority of classrooms)	Classroom Summary Form	
	4. Are the agreed-on rules incorporated into a matrix of classroom rules for classroom routines (e.g., arrival, free play, circle, snack) in classrooms? (*0* = no rules established or no; *1* = half or less than half; *2* = majority of classrooms)	Classroom Summary Form	
B. Behavioral Expectations Taught	1. Have lead teachers planned to teach the agreed-on rules in large- and/or small-group lessons? (*0* = no rules established or no; *1* = half or less than half; *2* = majority of lead teachers)	Classroom Summary Form	
	2. Can teachers state the agreed-on rules? (*0* = no rules established or no; *1* = half or less than half; *2* = majority of classroom teachers could state most of the rules)	Classroom Summary Form	
	3. Can children state the agreed-on rules? (*0* = no rules established or no; *1* = half or less than half; *2* = majority of classrooms had children who could state most of the rules)	Classroom Summary Form	
C. Responses to Appropriate and Challenging Behavior	1. Does the program have a system for acknowledging children's appropriate behavior (e.g., special spotlight or raffle, tokens for children who clean up) that is frequently used? (*0* = no; *1* = yes, implemented once a day; *2* = yes, implemented more than once a day	Administrator Interview Form	
	2. Do teachers implement the program's system for acknowledging children's appropriate behavior? (*0* = no system or no; *1* = half or less than half; *2* = majority of teachers)	Classroom Summary Form	

(page 1 of 4)

Figure A.10.   Blank PreSET Scoring Guide.

Feature	Evaluation question	Data source	Score (0, 1, 2)
C. Responses to Appropriate and Challenging Behavior *(continued)*	3. Does the program have a procedure for responding to children's challenging behavior that is hierarchical and function based (e.g., restate classroom rule, redirection to another activity, reteach skill, removal from area)? (*0* = no; *1* = yes, but procedure is basic; *2* = yes)	Administrator Interview Form	
	4. Do teachers consistently implement the program's procedure for responding to children's challenging behavior? (*0* = no procedure or no; *1* = half or less than half; *2* = majority of teachers)	Classroom Summary Form	
	5. Do teachers use at least a ratio of four positive statements (e.g., praise, approval) to each negative statement (e.g., reprimand, correction, disapproval)? (*0* = no; *1* = half or less than half; *2* = majority of teachers)	Classroom Summary Form	
	6. Do teachers use specific verbal praise at least once (e.g., "You used your walking feet")? (*0* = no; *1* = half or less than half; *2* = majority of teachers)	Classroom Summary Form	
	7. Do teachers use pre-correction (e.g., remind a child of a classroom rule in the absence of misbehavior)? (*0* = no; *1* = half or less than half; *2* = majority of teachers)	Classroom Summary Form	
D. Organized and Predictable Environment	1. Do classrooms have a schedule that includes visual pictures posted at children's eye level on at least one wall? (*0* = no; *1* = half or less than half; *2* = majority of classrooms)	Classroom Summary Form	
	2. Can teachers state what happens after a particular activity (e.g., what happens after circle time)? (*0* = no; *1* = half or less than half; *2* = majority of teachers)	Classroom Summary Form	
	3. Can children state what happens after a particular activity (e.g., what happens after circle time)? (*0* = no; *1* = half or less than half; *2* = majority of classrooms had children who could state what happens next)	Classroom Summary Form	
	4. Do teachers utilize a transition signal prior to transitions (e.g., ring bell, hand motion, sing song)? (*0* = no; *1* = half or less than half; *2* = majority of teachers)	Classroom Summary Form	
	5. Do teachers provide a verbal notice before the transition signal for choice, free, and outside play routines (e.g., "play time over in 2 minutes")? (*0* = no; *1* = half or less than half; *2* = majority of teachers)	Classroom Summary Form	
E. Monitoring and Decision Making	1. Does the program have a data collection form that is used daily to document children's challenging behavior? (*0* = no; *1* = yes, but not used daily or anecdotal report only; *2* = yes)	Administrator Interview Form	
	2. Is the program's data collection form for documenting children's challenging behavior being used in classrooms? (*0* = no form or no; *1* = half or less than half; *2* = majority of classrooms)	Classroom Summary Form	
	3. Does the program have a system (e.g., software, data entry person, time) that is used at least monthly for inputting data on children's challenging behavior? (*0* = no system or data not entered; *1* = yes, but system used less than monthly; *2* = yes, system used at least monthly)	Administrator Interview Form	

(page 2 of 4)

PreSET.

Feature	Evaluation question	Data source	Score (0, 1, 2)
E. **Monitoring and Decision Making** *(continued)*	4. Does the program have a system for reviewing data on children's challenging behavior for decision making? (*0 =* no system or data not reviewed; *1 =* yes, but data reviewed less than monthly; *2 =* yes, data reviewed at least monthly)	Administrator Interview Form	
F. **Family Involvement**	1. Do teachers communicate with families regularly? (*0 =* no; *1 =* half or less than half; *2 =* majority of teachers communicate with families in addition to drop off and pick up)	Classroom Summary Form	
	2. Do families participate in some way in each classroom? (*0 =* no; *1 =* half or less than half; *2 =* majority of classrooms)	Classroom Summary Form	
	3. Were families included in the development and/or revision of program expectations? (*0 =* no expectations or families not included; *2 =* yes)	Administrator Interview Form	
	4. Are families notified of program expectations in writing at least annually? (*0 =* no expectations or families not notified; *1 =* yes, but not in writing; *2 =* yes)	Administrator Interview Form	
	5. Are families notified of PW-PBIS strategies (e.g., how teachers teach social skills or respond to challenging behavior) in writing at least annually? *(0 =* no; *1 =* yes, but not in writing; *2 =* yes)	Administrator Interview Form	
G. **Management**	1. Is there an established team to address PW-PBIS (e.g., teaching and acknowledging behavioral expectations, developing a system for responding to challenging behavior)? (*0 =* no; *2 =* yes)	Administrator Interview Form	
	2. If a team is established, can teachers identify the function of the team? (*0 =* no team established or could not identify function; *1 =* half or less than half; *2 =* majority of teachers could identify the function of the PW-PBIS team)	Classroom Summary Form	
	3. Does the PW-PBIS team include appropriate members (e.g., classroom teacher, administrator, someone with behavioral/social skills expertise, someone with family/community knowledge)? (*0 =* no team established; *1 =* missing members; *2 =* yes)	Administrator Interview Form	
	4. Do PW-PBIS team meetings occur at least monthly? (*0 =* no team or no meeting; *1 =* less than monthly; *2 =* yes)	Administrator Interview Form	
	5. Does the program report progress related to PW-PBIS goals to all program staff at least twice a year? (*0 =* no team or reports less than once a year; *1 =* reports once a year; *2 =* yes)	Administrator Interview Form	
	6. Does the PW-PBIS team have an action plan with specific goals related to PW-PBIS that is less than one year old? (*0 =* no team or no action plan; *1 =* action plan older than one year; *2 =* yes)	Administrator Interview Form	

(page 3 of 4)

PreSET

Feature	Evaluation question	Data source	Score (0, 1, 2)
H. Program Support	1. Does the program have a budget with sufficient funds for building and maintaining PW-PBIS? *(0 = no; 1 = budget established, but insufficient funds; 2 = yes)*	Administrator Interview Form	
	2. Do program administrators report providing teachers with the time and resources (e.g., time to plan teaching lessons, money for rules posters) to implement goals related to PW-PBIS? *(0 = no; 1 = limited planning time or resources; 2 = yes)*	Administrator Interview Form	
	3. Has there been at least one recent professional development opportunity for staff related to PW-PBIS? *(0 = no; 1 = yes, but it was over a year ago; 2 = yes)*	Administrator Interview Form	
	4. Do teachers report having sufficient time and access to resources to implement goals related to PW-PBIS? *(0 = no; 1 = half or less than half; 2 = majority of teachers)*	Classroom Summary Form	

PreSET program summary scores

Summary scores	A Expectations Defined	B Behavioral Expectations Taught	C Responses to Appropriate and Challenging Behavior	D Organized and Predictable Environment	E Monitoring and Decision Making	F Family Involvement	G Management	H Program Support
	/ 8	/ 6	/ 14	/ 10	/ 8	/ 10	/ 12	/ 8
Percent implemented								

Total percent implemented all features:

_____ ÷ 8 = _____ % (Average percent implemented)

(page 4 of 4)

PreSET — Classroom Interview and Observation Form

Program: _Busy Bee Preschool_   Classroom: _Preschool 1_   Date: _9/15/10_

Teacher Questions

Interview up to three teachers

Respondent:	What are the program's rules? (B2) Record number known that match program's rules (Note: Automatically circle "no" if no program rules established.)		What happens after (circle time)? (D2) Must agree with posted classroom schedule and each other. Record + or –
	Number Known	Number of Rules	
Teacher 1	3	3	+
Teacher 2	2	3	+
Teacher 3			
Scoring	Did all interviewed teachers state the majority of the program rules? (Yes) No		Did all interviewed teachers correctly state what happens after (circle time)? (Yes) No

Children's Questions

A teacher should ask three children the following two questions. Use verbal prompting and accommodations for children's language abilities as necessary.

Respondent:	What are the rules in your classroom? (B3) Record number known that match program's rules (Note: Automatically circle "no" if no program rules established.)		What happens after (circle time)? (D3) Must agree with posted classroom schedule and teachers. Record + or –
	Number Known	Number of Rules	
Child 1	2	3	+
Child 2	3	3	+
Child 3	3	3	+
Scoring	Did all interviewed children state the majority of the classroom rules? (Yes) No		Did all interviewed children correctly state what happens after (circle time)? (Yes) No

Lead Teacher Questions

How do you teach the program rules in your classroom? (B1) (Note: Automatically circle "no" if no program rules established.)	How do you acknowledge appropriate behavior? (C2) (Note: Automatically circle "no" if no system identified by administrator.)	How do you respond to challenging behavior? (C4) (Note: Automatically circle "no" if no procedure identified by administrator.)	What do you use to collect data on children's challenging behavior? (E2) (Note: Automatically circle "no" if no data form identified by administrator.)
Review and sing rules during circle time using a Bee puppet; focus on the key Buzz word each month.	The children can earn bee stickers to add to the hive on the bulletin board.	Either redirect or talk about the issue, problem solve, and practice a new solution; some behaviors are tracked on a form.	Behavior incident form.
Program rules are taught in large or small groups? Yes* (No) *Must see a lesson plan to score "yes"	Is there a system? (Yes) No *The system must match the program's and you must observe its use or evidence of its use to score "yes"	Is there a procedure? (Yes) No *The procedure must match the program's and you must observe its use or evidence of its use to score "yes"	Data collection form? (Yes*) No *The form must match the program's form and you must observe its use or evidence of its use to score "yes"

How do you communicate with families? (F1)	How do families participate in the classroom? (F2)	(If there is a PBS team) What is the function of the program's PBS team? (G2) (Note: Automatically circle "no" if no program-wide PBS team established.)	Do you have sufficient time for planning and enough resources to meet your teaching goals? (H4)
Daily at drop off and pick up, monthly newsletters, e-mail, parent conferences 2 x per year, phone calls as needed.	Some parents will come in and have lunch with their children; field trip volunteers, provide requested supplies, read a story to the children.	They create, change, and add to the program Behavior Curriculum to keep consistency in each classroom, determine skills to focus on monthly for teaching rules.	Somewhat. I wish I had more planning time. I get supplies I need.
Communicate with families? (Yes*) No *Must include at least one other way besides pick up and drop off to score "yes" (e.g., e-mail, phone, home visits)	Families participate in the classroom (e.g., classroom helpers, readers)? (Yes) No	(If there is a PBS team) Correct function of the PW-PBS team? (Yes) No	Sufficient planning time and adequate resources? Yes (No)

Figure A.11. Fully completed PreSET Classroom Interview and Observation Form for Classroom 1.

Figure A.11. *(continued)*

Classroom Environment

Use the items in italics to score the presence or absence of the following items in the classroom. *(Note: Automatically circle "no" for A2, A3, and A4 if no program rules established.)*

Are program rules posted in at least one classroom location at eye level? *Wall poster(s)* (A2)	Do program rules include a combination of words and visuals? *Wall poster(s)* (A3)	Are program rules incorporated into a matrix of expectations for classroom routines? *Matrix of classroom rules* (A4)	Is there a posted classroom schedule that includes visual pictures at eye level for children on at least one wall? *Classroom schedule* (D1)
(Yes) No	(Yes) No	(Yes) No	Yes (No)

10-minute Classroom Observation

Observe during a classroom routine such as free play, circle time, or snack; choose one teacher to observe.
Time started: 9:05   Time ended: 9:15

Tally the number of positive statements (praise, approval) (C5)	Tally the number of negative statements (reprimand, correction, disapproval) (C5)	Tally the number of comments using specific verbal praise (C6)
////	/	///
Divide the number of positive statements by the number of negative statements: 4/1 = 4.0 *Is the result a number of 4.0 or greater?* (Yes) No		*Was there at least 1?* (Yes) No

Transition

Observe at least one transition from an unstructured or less structured activity (e.g., free play, outside) to a more structured activity (e.g., circle time, snack time).

Did at least one teacher use pre-correction (e.g., remind a child of a classroom rule in the absence of misbehavior) at least once? (C7)	Did at least one teacher use a system other than or in addition to a verbal direction to signal the transition (e.g., ring bell, hand motion, sing song)? (D4)	Did at least one teacher provide a notice before the transition signal (e.g., play time over in 2 minutes)? (D5)
///	(Yes) No	Yes (No)

Notes:

Classroom schedule posted with pictures but not at eye level for children.

PreSET Classroom Interview and Observation Form

Program: _Busy Bee Preschool_   Classroom: _Preschool 2_   Date: _9/15/10_

Teacher Questions
Interview up to three teachers

Respondent:	What are the program's rules? (B2) Record number known that match program's rules (Note: Automatically circle "no" if no program rules established.)		What happens after (circle time)? (D2) Must agree with posted classroom schedule and each other. Record + or –
	Number Known	Number of Rules	
Teacher 1	3		+
Teacher 2	2	3	–
Teacher 3			
Scoring	Did all interviewed teachers state the majority of the program rules? Yes (No)		Did all interviewed teachers correctly state what happens after (circle time)? Yes (No)

Children's Questions
A teacher should ask three children the following two questions. Use verbal prompting and accommodations for children's language abilities as necessary.

Respondent:	What are the rules in your classroom? (B3) Record number known that match program's rules (Note: Automatically circle "no" if no program rules established.)		What happens after (circle time)? (D3) Must agree with posted classroom schedule and teachers.
	Number Known	Number of Rules	Record + or –
Child 1	3	3	+
Child 2	2	3	–
Child 3	2	3	–
Scoring	Did all interviewed children state the majority of the classroom rules? (Yes) No		Did all interviewed children correctly state what happens after (circle time)? Yes (No)

Lead Teacher Questions

How do you teach the program rules in your classroom? (B1) (Note: Automatically circle "no" if no program rules established.)	How do you acknowledge appropriate behavior? (C2) (Note: Automatically circle "no" if no system identified by administrator.)	How do you respond to challenging behavior? (C4) (Note: Automatically circle "no" if no procedure identified by administrator.)	What do you use to collect data on children's challenging behavior? (E2) (Note: Automatically circle "no" if no data form identified by administrator.)	How do you communicate with families? (F1)	How do families participate in the classroom? (F2)	(If there is a PBS team) What is the function of the program's PBS team? (G2) (Note: Automatically circle "no" if no program-wide PBS team established.)	Do you have sufficient time for planning and enough resources to meet your teaching goals? (H4)
Sing rules every day at circle time with puppets.	I give the children Bee stickers for the class Beehive, then when the Hive is full, we have a class party.	Try to redirect whenever possible, then talk with the child at his or her level, practice a new skill for next time it occurs, sometimes document if needed.	Behavior incident form.	Each day when they drop off and pick up their child, sometimes phone calls, e-mail, monthly newsletter.	They volunteer for field trips, help with class supplies—most are working so we don't see them a lot in the classroom. The same ones volunteer all of the time.	They come up with skills for us to focus on during circle and review our behavior data; they work on improving the data system and getting us to consistently use it.	Sort of. We never get time to lesson plan but I usually always get what I want for materials and I get reimbursed if I get it on my own.
Program rules are taught in large or small groups? Yes* (No) *Must see a lesson plan to score "yes"	Is there a system? (Yes)* No *The system must match the program's and you must observe its use or evidence of its use to score "yes"	Is there a procedure? (Yes)* No *The procedure must match the program's and you must observe its use or evidence of its use to score "yes"	Data collection form? (Yes)* No *The form must match the program's form and you must observe its use or evidence of its use to score "yes"	Communicate with families? (Yes)* No *Must include at least one other way besides pick up and drop off to score "yes" (e.g., e-mail, phone, home visits)	Families participate in the classroom (e.g., classroom helpers, readers)? (Yes)* No	(If there is a PBS team) Correct function of the PW-PBS team? (Yes) No	Sufficient planning time and adequate resources? Yes (No)

Figure A.12.   Fully completed PreSET Classroom Interview and Observation Form for Classroom 2.

Figure A.12. (continued)

PreSET

Classroom Environment

Use the items in italics to score the presence or absence of the following items in the classroom. (Note: Automatically circle "no" for A2, A3, and A4 if no program rules established.)

Are program rules posted in at least one classroom location at eye level? *Wall poster(s) (A2)*	Do program rules include a combination of words and visuals? *Wall poster(s) (A3)*	Are program rules incorporated into a matrix of expectations for classroom routines? *Matrix of classroom rules (A4)*	Is there a posted classroom schedule that includes visual pictures at eye level for children on at least one wall? *Classroom schedule (D1)*
(Yes) No	(Yes) No	(Yes) No	Yes (No)

10-minute Classroom Observation

Observe during a classroom routine such as free play, circle time, or snack; choose one teacher to observe.
Time started: 9:35   Time ended: 9:45

Tally the number of positive statements (praise, approval) (C5)	Tally the number of negative statements (reprimand, correction, disapproval) (C5)	Tally the number of comments using specific verbal praise (C6)
///	//	/
Divide the number of positive statements by the number of negative statements: 3/2 = 1.5 *Is the result a number of 4.0 or greater?* Yes (No)		*Was there at least 1?* (Yes) No

Transition

Observe at least one transition from an unstructured or less structured activity (e.g., free play, outside) to a more structured activity (e.g., circle time, snack time).

Did at least one teacher use pre-correction (e.g., remind a child of a classroom rule in the absence of misbehavior) at least once? (C7)	Did at least one teacher use a system other than or in addition to a verbal direction to signal the transition (e.g., ring bell, hand motion, sing song)? (D4)	Did at least one teacher provide a notice before the transition signal (e.g., play time over in 2 minutes)? (D5)
Yes (No)	Yes (No)	(Yes) No

Notes:

Classroom schedule does not have pictures.
Assistant teacher has been working in this classroom for 8 weeks.

PreSET — Classroom Interview and Observation Form

Program: _Busy Bee Preschool_   Classroom: _Preschool 3_   Date: _9/15/10_

Teacher Questions
Interview up to three teachers

Respondent:	What are the program's rules? (B2) Record number known that match program's rules (Note: Automatically circle "no" if no program rules established.)		What happens after (circle time)? (D2) Must agree with posted classroom schedule and each other. Record + or –
	Number Known	Number of Rules	
Teacher 1	2	3	– (no schedule posted)
Teacher 2	1	3	–
Teacher 3	0	3	–
Scoring	Did all interviewed teachers state the majority of the program rules? Yes (No)		Did all interviewed teachers correctly state what happens after (circle time)? Yes (No)

Children's Questions
A teacher should ask three children the following two questions. Use verbal prompting and accommodations for children's language abilities as necessary.

Respondent:	What are the rules in your classroom? (B3) Record number known that match program's rules (Note: Automatically circle "no" if no program rules established.)		What happens after (circle time)? (D3) Must agree with posted classroom schedule and teachers. Record + or –
	Number Known	Number of Rules	
Child 1	1	3	–
Child 2	0	3	–
Child 3	1	3	–
Scoring	Did all interviewed children state the majority of the classroom rules? Yes (No)		Did all interviewed children correctly state what happens after (circle time)? Yes (No)

Lead Teacher Questions

How do you teach the program rules in your classroom? (B1) (Note: Automatically circle "no" if no program rules established.)	How do you acknowledge appropriate behavior? (C2) (Note: Automatically circle "no" if no system identified by administrator.)	How do you respond to challenging behavior? (C4) (Note: Automatically circle "no" if no procedure identified by administrator.)	What do you use to collect data on children's challenging behavior? (E2) (Note: Automatically circle "no" if no data form identified by administrator.)	How do you communicate with families? (F1)	(If there is a PBS team) What is the function of the program's PBS team? (G2) (Note: Automatically circle "no" if no program-wide PBS team established.)	Do you have sufficient time for planning and enough resources to meet your teaching goals? (H4)
I go over the rules poster at circle time everyday (pointed to the rules poster) – five rules that do not match program rules.	I give lots of praise and high fives. We have Bee stickers for the Hive, but I don't use that. I use it sometimes for GREAT behavior only.	I usually just use the time-out strategy for most issues. Sometimes I remove an item or take away an activity.	I keep notes in a note-book for major incidents and share it with parents when they pick up their child.	When they drop off and pick up their child. I spend more time talking to them at pick up probably.	I think there's a team that meets, but I don't know what they do.	I never have time to plan lessons or activities. I do that at home.
Program rules are taught in large or small groups? Yes* (No) *Must see lesson plan to score "yes"	Is there a system? Yes* (No) *The system must match the program's and you must observe its use or evidence of its use to score "yes"	Is there a procedure? Yes* (No) *The procedure must match the program's and you must observe its use or evidence of its use to score "yes"	Data collection form? Yes* (No) *The form must match the program's form and you must observe its use or evidence of its use to score "yes"	Communicate with families? Yes* (No) *Must include at least one other way besides pick up and drop off to score "yes" (e.g., e-mail, phone, home visits)	(If there is a PBS team) Correct function of the PW-PBS team? Yes (No)	Sufficient planning time and adequate resources? Yes (No)

How do families participate in the classroom? (F2)	Families participate in the classroom (e.g., classroom helpers, readers)?
These families work so they don't come into the classroom.	Yes (No)

Figure A.13. Fully completed PreSET Classroom Interview and Observation Form for Classroom 3.

Figure A.13. *(continued)*

Classroom Environment

Use the items in italics to score the presence or absence of the following items in the classroom. (*Note: Automatically circle "no" for A2, A3, and A4 if no program rules established.*)

Are program rules posted in at least one classroom location at eye level? *Wall poster(s) (A2)*	Do program rules include a combination of words and visuals? *Wall poster(s) (A3)*	Are program rules incorporated into a matrix of expectations for classroom routines? *Matrix of classroom rules (A4)*	Is there a posted classroom schedule that includes visual pictures at eye level for children on at least one wall? *Classroom schedule (D1)*
Yes (No)	Yes (No)	(Yes) No	Yes (No)

10-minute Classroom Observation

Observe during a classroom routine such as free play, circle time, or snack; choose one teacher to observe.
Time started: 9:55   Time ended: 10:05

Tally the number of positive statements (praise, approval) (C5)	Tally the number of negative statements (reprimand, correction, disapproval) (C5)	Tally the number of comments using specific verbal praise (C6)
II	III	I

Divide the number of positive statements by the number of negative statements:

$$\frac{2/3}{} = 0.67$$

Is the result a number of 4.0 or greater?
Yes (No)

Was there at least 1?
(Yes) No

Transition

Observe at least one transition from an unstructured or less structured activity (e.g., free play, outside) to a more structured activity (e.g., circle time, snack time).

Did at least one teacher use precorrection (e.g., remind a child of a classroom rule in the absence of misbehavior) at least once? (C7)	Did at least one teacher use a system other than or in addition to a verbal direction to signal the transition (e.g., ring bell, hand motion, sing song)? (D4)	Did at least one teacher provide a notice before the transition signal (e.g., play time over in 2 minutes)? (D5)
Yes (No)	Yes (No)	(Yes) No

Notes:

All new teachers. Lead teacher has been there 3 months. Assistant teacher 1 has been there 2 months. Assistant teacher 2 was a new position added to the program 3 weeks ago due to parent complaints regarding behavioral concerns in the classroom.

⊗ PreSET

Classroom Summary Form

Instructions: For a given program, transfer each classroom's scores from the Classroom Interview and Observation Form. Note the score as Y (yes) or N (no). When all participating classrooms' scores are transferred, complete the summary indicating a 0, 1, or 2 score.

Classroom	Classroom 1	Classroom 2	Classroom 3	Classroom 4	Classroom 5	Classroom 6	Classroom 7	Classroom 8	Classroom 9	Classroom 10		Summary: (0 = No for all; 1 = Yes for half or less than half; 2 = Yes for majority)
Teachers state rules (B2)	Y	Y	N								B2	2
Teachers state what happens next (D2)	Y	N	N								D2	1
Children state rules (B3)	Y	Y	N								B3	2
Children state what happens next (D3)	Y	N	N								D3	1
Plan to teach classroom rules (B1)	N	N	N								B1	0
System to acknowledge appropriate behavior (C2)	Y	Y	N								C2	2
System for responding to challenging behavior (C4)	Y	Y	N								C4	0
Data collection form (E2)	Y	Y	N								E2	2
Communicate with families in at least one way *in addition to* drop off/pick up (F1)	Y	Y	N								F1	2
Families participate in classroom (F2)	Y	Y	N								F2	2
Correct function of PW-PBIS team (G2)	Y	Y	N								G2	2
Sufficient time and access to resources (H4)	N	N	N								H4	0
Rules posted at eye level (A2)	Y	Y	N								A2	2
Rules include words and visuals (A3)	Y	Y	N								A3	2
Matrix of classroom rules (A4)	Y	Y	Y								A4	2
Schedule with visual pictures at eye level (D1)	N	N	N								D1	0
Ratio of 4:1 positive to negative statements (C5)	Y	N	N								C5	1
Specific verbal praise (C6)	Y	Y	Y								C6	2
Precorrection during transition (C7)	Y	N	N								C7	1
Transition signal (D4)	Y	N	N								D4	1
Notice before transition signal (D5)	N	Y	Y								D5	2

Figure A.14.   Completed PreSET Classroom Summary Form.

 **Scoring Guide**

Directions: Transfer information obtained from the PreSET Administrator Interview Form and PreSET Classroom Summary Form to this scoring guide to determine the program's PreSET total score and percent implemented by feature. Each item on this scoring guide should be scored with a *0, 1,* or *2* according to the guidelines outlined in the evaluation question description.

Please see the PreSET Administrator Interview Form and PreSET Classroom Interview and Observation Form for directions on how to conduct interviews and observations with the program administrator, staff, and children.

Program: _Busy Bee Preschool_   Date: _9/15/10_

Administrator: _C. Smith_   Date of last PreSET and score: _9/8/09_

City, State: _Some City, Some State_   Number of classrooms: _3_

PreSET data collector(s): _B. Harris_

Notes: _Several new teachers since the last PreSET as noted on the administrator interview form._

Feature	Evaluation question	Data source	Score (0, 1, 2)
A. Expectations Defined	1. Has the program agreed to five or fewer positively stated expectations? (*0* = no; *1* = yes, but more than five, negatively stated, and/or classrooms have their own expectations; *2* = yes)	Administrator Interview Form	2
	2. Are the agreed-on rules publicly posted at children's eye level in classrooms? (*0* = no rules established or no; *1* = half or less than half; *2* = majority of classrooms)	Classroom Summary Form	2
	3. Are the agreed-on rules posted with a combination of words and visuals in classrooms? (*0* = no rules established or no; *1* = half or less than half; *2* = majority of classrooms)	Classroom Summary Form	2
	4. Are the agreed-on rules incorporated into a matrix of classroom rules for classroom routines (e.g., arrival, free play, circle, snack) in classrooms? (*0* = no rules established or no; *1* = half or less than half; *2* = majority of classrooms)	Classroom Summary Form	2
B. Behavioral Expectations Taught	1. Have lead teachers planned to teach the agreed-on rules in large- and/or small-group lessons? (*0* = no rules established or no; *1* = half or less than half; *2* = majority of lead teachers)	Classroom Summary Form	0
	2. Can teachers state the agreed-on rules? (*0* = no rules established or no; *1* = half or less than half; *2* = majority of classroom teachers could state most of the rules)	Classroom Summary Form	2
	3. Can children state the agreed-on rules? (*0* = no rules established or no; *1* = half or less than half; *2* = majority of classrooms had children who could state most of the rules)	Classroom Summary Form	2
C. Responses to Appropriate and Challenging Behavior	1. Does the program have a system for acknowledging children's appropriate behavior (e.g., special spotlight or raffle, tokens for children who clean up) that is frequently used? (*0* = no; *1* = yes, implemented once a day; *2* = yes, implemented more than once a day)	Administrator Interview Form	1
	2. Do teachers implement the program's system for acknowledging children's appropriate behavior? (*0* = no system or no; *1* = half or less than half; *2* = majority of teachers)	Classroom Summary Form	2

(page 1 of 4)

Figure A.15.   Completed PreSET Scoring Guide.

PreSET

Feature	Evaluation question	Data source	Score (0, 1, 2)
C. Responses to Appropriate and Challenging Behavior *(continued)*	3. Does the program have a procedure for responding to children's challenging behavior that is hierarchical and function based (e.g., restate classroom rule, redirection to another activity, reteach skill, removal from area)? (*0* = no; *1* = yes, but procedure is basic; *2* = yes)	Administrator Interview Form	2
	4. Do teachers consistently implement the program's procedure for responding to children's challenging behavior? (*0* = no procedure or no; *1* = half or less than half; *2* = majority of teachers)	Classroom Summary Form	2
	5. Do teachers use at least a ratio of four positive statements (e.g., praise, approval) to each negative statement (e.g., reprimand, correction, disapproval)? (*0* = no; *1* = half or less than half; *2* = majority of teachers)	Classroom Summary Form	1
	6. Do teachers use specific verbal praise at least once (e.g., "You used your walking feet")? (*0* = no; *1* = half or less than half; *2* = majority of teachers)	Classroom Summary Form	2
	7. Do teachers use pre-correction (e.g., remind a child of a classroom rule in the absence of misbehavior)? (*0* = no; *1* = half or less than half; *2* = majority of teachers)	Classroom Summary Form	1
D. Organized and Predictable Environment	1. Do classrooms have a schedule that includes visual pictures posted at children's eye level on at least one wall? (*0* = no; *1* = half or less than half; *2* = majority of classrooms)	Classroom Summary Form	*0*
	2. Can teachers state what happens after a particular activity (e.g., what happens after circle time)? (*0* = no; *1* = half or less than half; *2* = majority of teachers)	Classroom Summary Form	1
	3. Can children state what happens after a particular activity (e.g., what happens after circle time)? (*0* = no; *1* = half or less than half; *2* = majority of classrooms had children who could state what happens next)	Classroom Summary Form	1
	4. Do teachers utilize a transition signal prior to transitions (e.g., ring bell, hand motion, sing song)? (*0* = no; *1* = half or less than half; *2* = majority of teachers)	Classroom Summary Form	1
	5. Do teachers provide a verbal notice before the transition signal for choice, free, and outside play routines (e.g., "play time over in 2 minutes")? (*0* = no; *1* = half or less than half; *2* = majority of teachers)	Classroom Summary Form	2
E. Monitoring and Decision Making	1. Does the program have a data collection form that is used daily to document children's challenging behavior? (*0* = no; *1* = yes, but not used daily or anecdotal report only; *2* = yes)	Administrator Interview Form	2
	2. Is the program's data collection form for documenting children's challenging behavior being used in classrooms? (*0* = no form or no; *1* = half or less than half; *2* = majority of classrooms)	Classroom Summary Form	2
	3. Does the program have a system (e.g., software, data entry person, time) that is used at least monthly for inputting data on children's challenging behavior? (*0* = no system or data not entered; *1* = yes, but system used less than monthly; *2* = yes, system used at least monthly)	Administrator Interview Form	2

(page 2 of 4)

PreSET

Feature	Evaluation question	Data source	Score (0, 1, 2)
E. **Monitoring and Decision Making** *(continued)*	4. Does the program have a system for reviewing data on children's challenging behavior for decision making? (*0* = no system or data not reviewed; *1* = yes, but data reviewed less than monthly; *2* = yes, data reviewed at least monthly)	Administrator Interview Form	1
F. **Family Involvement**	1. Do teachers communicate with families regularly? (*0* = no; *1* = half or less than half; *2* = majority of teachers communicate with families in addition to drop off and pick up)	Classroom Summary Form	2
	2. Do families participate in some way in each classroom? (*0* = no; *1* = half or less than half; *2* = majority of classrooms)	Classroom Summary Form	2
	3. Were families included in the development and/or revision of program expectations? (*0* = no expectations or families not included; *2* = yes)	Administrator Interview Form	2
	4. Are families notified of program expectations in writing at least annually? (*0* = no expectations or families not notified; *1* = yes, but not in writing; *2* = yes)	Administrator Interview Form	2
	5. Are families notified of PW-PBIS strategies (e.g., how teachers teach social skills or respond to challenging behavior) in writing at least annually? (*0* = no; *1* = yes, but not in writing; *2* = yes)	Administrator Interview Form	2
G. **Management**	1. Is there an established team to address PW-PBIS (e.g., teaching and acknowledging behavioral expectations, developing a system for responding to challenging behavior)? (*0* = no; *2* = yes)	Administrator Interview Form	2
	2. If a team is established, can teachers identify the function of the team? (*0* = no team established or could not identify function; *1* = half or less than half; *2* = majority of teachers could identify the function of the PW-PBIS team)	Classroom Summary Form	2
	3. Does the PW-PBIS team include appropriate members (e.g., classroom teacher, administrator, someone with behavioral/social skills expertise, someone with family/community knowledge)? (*0* = no team established; *1* = missing members; *2* = yes)	Administrator Interview Form	2
	4. Do PW-PBIS team meetings occur at least monthly? (*0* = no team or no meeting; *1* = less than monthly; *2* = yes)	Administrator Interview Form	2
	5. Does the team report progress related to PW-PBIS goals to all program staff at least twice a year? (*0* = no team or reports less than once a year; *1* = reports once a year; *2* = yes)	Administrator Interview Form	2
	6. Does the PW-PBIS team have an action plan with specific goals related to PW-PBIS that is less than one year old? (*0* = no team or no action plan; *1* = action plan older than one year; *2* = yes)	Administrator Interview Form	0

(page 3 of 4)

Feature	Evaluation question	Data source	Score (0, 1, 2)
H. Program Support	1. Does the program have a budget with sufficient funds for building and maintaining PW-PBIS? *(0 = no; 1 = budget established, but insufficient funds; 2 = yes)*	Administrator Interview Form	2
	2. Do program administrators report providing teachers with the time and resources (e.g., time to plan teaching lessons, money for rules posters) to implement goals related to PW-PBIS? (0 = no; *1 = limited planning time or resources; 2 = yes)*	Administrator Interview Form	1
	3. Has there been at least one recent professional development opportunity for staff related to PW-PBIS? *(0 = no; 1 = yes, but it was over a year ago; 2 = yes)*	Administrator Interview Form	2
	4. Do teachers report having sufficient time and access to resources to implement goals related to PW-PBIS? (0 = no; *1 = half or less than half; 2 = majority of teachers)*	Classroom Summary Form	0

PreSET program summary scores

Summary scores	A Expectations Defined	B Behavioral Expectations Taught	C Responses to Appropriate and Challenging Behavior	D Organized and Predictable Environment	E Monitoring and Decision Making	F Family Involvement	G Management	H Program Support
	8 / 8	4 / 6	11 / 14	5 / 10	7 / 8	10 / 10	10 / 12	5 / 8
Percent implemented	100%	67%	79%	50%	88%	100%	83%	63%

Total percent implemented all features:	630	÷	8	=	79	%	(Average percent implemented)

(page 4 of 4)

Frequently Asked Questions

PREPARING FOR THE PreSET

Do I need consent to interview early childhood staff and children?

You do not need to solicit consent unless you are using the PreSET for research purposes. In this case, district-level consent is necessary, as well as any institutional consent (e.g., institutional review board) that is required at your institution.

What do I need to have completed before I arrive at the school?

You will conduct all interviews and observations during your visit to the school. First, be sure to arrange the PreSET with relevant program staff and ask them to have any materials ready for your review. Also be sure to bring copies of all the required forms to conduct the PreSET, including the PreSET Administrator Interview Form (one copy) and the Classroom Interview and Observation Form (one copy per classroom). The Classroom Summary Form and PreSET Scoring Guide will only be necessary at the time of scoring, but you may want to have all materials with you on the scheduled date of the PreSET (at your own discretion and per personal preference).

Do I need to interview the administrator first?

Ideally, you should interview the administrator first. However, if this is not possible, you may find out what the program's expectations and systems of acknowledgment (if they exist) are and then complete the classroom observations before speaking to the administrator.

CONDUCTING THE PreSET

What should I do if the children in the classroom do not have sufficient language and/or cognitive skills to participate in the classroom interviews?

Attempts should be made to provide adaptations (e.g., use of alternative methods of communication) for children to respond to classroom interviews in the manner that suits them. However, if this is not possible, evaluators may use observation of children's behavioral responses to teacher's prompts, transitions, and schedule changes (e.g., all children move as a group immediately after a transition signal, children anticipate the next activity by obtaining materials without a teacher prompt, children follow classroom rules without reminders) to note information that would otherwise be obtained by having the teacher interview the children.

If the classroom is very small (e.g., fewer than five children), do I still need to interview three children? On the other hand, if the classroom is very large (e.g., 24 children), do I need to only interview three children?

You should use your best judgment on obtaining a representative sample of children from the classroom to interview. If the classroom is really small (e.g., fewer than five children), you may need to only interview two children to provide you with enough information to confidently score the items on the PreSET Classroom Interview and Observation Form. Alternatively, if the classroom is exceptionally large (e.g., 24 children), you may interview more than three children—but this is not required.

How should the teacher choose which children to interview?

The teacher may select which three children that he or she would like to interview. It often makes sense to choose children who are engaged in tasks that allow them to be pulled aside for the brief interview more easily. The teacher may also wish to choose children who are more likely to be responsive to an interview.

What if there is a new teacher, family member, volunteer, or student teacher visiting the classroom during PreSET administration? Should I include him or her in my interviews and observations?

New teachers (on staff less than 2 weeks), family members, volunteers, and student teachers should not be included as "staff" for staff interviews and observations. However, if these individuals are willing to answer questions and participate in the PreSET process, they may be included informally.

What if I conduct the PreSET on a hectic day and the staff are not able to show me materials they say they have (e.g., program handbook)?

Make arrangements for the program administrator to send you the materials via e-mail or postal mail. If this is not possible, use the information that you obtained during PreSET administration to score the forms and scoring guide.

SCORING THE PreSET

How do I score items that pertain to having a systemwide or program-wide practice if individual classrooms are implementing the feature, but it is not part of a systemwide or program-wide practice?

You should make a note of what the individual classrooms are doing but score the item as it was intended—as a program-wide indicator. The item should be scored as the PreSET is intended—as a measure of program-wide PBIS implementation of universal practices. However, your notes about what individual classrooms are doing may help the program recognize effective practices occurring in individual classrooms and move to adopting these practices program wide.

INTERPRETING AND SHARING THE RESULTS

What data should I provide to the program administrator?

Before you leave the program, you should share a few positive highlights of what you have discovered about the program's implementation of PW-PBIS features. You should tell the administrator that you will provide a more in-depth summary, including the program's scores on each of the eight features and the average percentage of features implemented, when you share the results with the PW-PBIS leadership team.

FOLLOW-UP

How do I determine how often to administer the PreSET?

To determine how often to administer the PreSET in a program, the evaluator must consider whether the program is just beginning PW-PBIS development or whether the program already has an established system of PW-PBIS in place. It is recommended that the PreSET be conducted before and after implementation to attain baseline information, establish action planning goals, and measure progress toward goal attainment.

A program that is just beginning PW-PBIS development should have the PreSET completed twice within the first year. For example, it can be completed once to obtain preimplementation data and determine an action plan, then again at the end of the program year to measure growth during the course of the year and determine action planning for the following year. If a program has been implementing PW-PBIS for over a year, the PreSET can be administered once yearly to monitor for fidelity of implementation and establish goals for the upcoming program year.

If the program administrator changes, should I administer an entirely new PreSET or just a new administrator interview? How long should I wait to do a new PreSET after a new administrator starts?

Administrative (or other staff) change within an early childhood program requires the establishment of PW-PBIS orientation procedures including professional development, training, and/or mentorship supports to help familiarize new staff with the current PW-PBIS practices within the program. This should occur prior to administering another PreSET within the program. Please also keep in mind that an adequate amount of time is needed for a new administrator (or other new staff) to learn a program's PW-PBIS systems and operations.

Programs that experience high administrative and/or other staff turnover are more susceptible to encountering challenges in attaining or maintaining fidelity of implementation on the PreSET. In particular, administrative change may result in PW-PBIS revisions and/or modifications within a program. Because scoring of the PreSET involves agreement between the administrator and program staff for many PreSET items, the staff responses are crucial for determining whether PW-PBIS practices are being adequately maintained. Therefore, it is recommended that the PreSET be readministered in its entirety as close to the typical program evaluation schedule as possible.

Once I have my PreSET scores, what do I do next? What do I offer the program in terms of increasing its score (if low) or maintaining its score (if high)?

Once the PreSET scores are finalized, use the sample Feedback Form in this manual as a tool to guide the written report and recommendations developed for the program. Be sure to address each feature, emphasizing both program-wide and individual classrooms' strengths and commendations as well as areas in need of improvement. It is often helpful to schedule a follow-up meeting with the administrator—or preferably with the program's PW-PBIS team—to review the PreSET results and determine goals for program improvement or maintenance.

If the PreSET score is initially low, be cognizant of and sensitive to the fact that some staff may defend current program practices. If there is disagreement with a particular item or feature score, explain the basis for the score and the evidence required for full score attainment (e.g., written documentation of teaching expectations on lesson plans). If new evidence is presented that validates the request for reconsideration of a score, it is acceptable to make adjustments in order to provide the most accurate score possible. In addition, be sure to address the availability of PW-PBIS consultation, technical assistance, or other such support services for continued improvement and sustainability of positive behavior support practices in early childhood settings.

The information that follows is designed to help you understand the rights and permissions associated with using PreSET.

PHOTOCOPYING

Can the PreSET forms be photocopied?

Yes, the PreSET forms (Administrator Interview Form, Classroom Interview and Observation Form, Classroom Summary Form, Scoring Guide, Feedback Form, and PW-PBIS Action Plan) may be photocopied for use at a single physical site or branch office. The photocopies must be made from a set of original forms printed from the CD-ROM.

POSTING

Can I post the PDF forms on the CD-ROM on my program's computer network?

It depends. The Administrator Interview Form, Classroom Interview and Observation Form, Classroom Summary Form, Scoring Guide, Feedback Form, and PW-PBIS Action Plan can be posted on your program's local area network (LAN) or intranet if *only* people in your organization at a single physical site or branch office have access to the LAN or intranet. Employees can then print and use the forms as needed from their own computers at that single physical site. Remote access from another physical site, including by virtual private network (VPN), file transfer protocol (FTP), tunneling protocols, or other means, is not permitted.

Can I post PreSET forms on my web site or my organization's web site?

No, posting PreSET forms on any web site, password protected or otherwise, is not permitted.

E-MAILING

Can I e-mail PreSET forms to a colleague or other individual?

No, blank forms may not be e-mailed to anyone for any reason. However, you may share *completed* forms with a program administrator after finishing a PreSET observation of that program.

EXTRACTING

Can I use some of the questions from PreSET in an item that I am creating?

Brookes Publishing appreciates interest in PreSET. However, you need written permission from Brookes Publishing before adapting, translating, reformatting, reprinting, or reproducing (except as covered by the PreSET Photocopying Release) the forms or any related material, or any part thereof in any way. To apply for permission, please complete a Permission Request Form online at http://www.brookespublishing.com

CD-ROM

How can I use the PreSET CD-ROM?

The CD-ROM contains the blank PreSET forms. You may print and photocopy the forms as needed under the terms specified in the Photocopying Release and the End User License Agreement (EULA) on the CD-ROM.

The PreSET Administrator Interview Form, Classroom Interview and Observation Form, Classroom Summary Form, Scoring Guide, Feedback Form, and PW-PBIS Action Plan can be posted on a local area network (LAN) or intranet. Only people in your organization at a single physical site or branch office can have access to the LAN or intranet, and they can access the materials only from that single physical site.

MORE INFORMATION

How do I get more information about PreSET usage and rights and permissions?

More information is available through the Brookes Publishing's Subsidiary Rights Department at rights@brookespublishing.com. E-mails are answered as quickly as possible. However, owing to the volume of inquiries received, please be advised that it may be approximately 4 to 6 weeks before you receive a response.

Technical Appendix

This technical appendix presents initial findings regarding the psychometric properties of the *Preschool-Wide Evaluation Tool™ (PreSET™), Research Edition*. The purpose of the PreSET is to measure fidelity of implementation of program-wide positive behavior intervention and support (PW-PBIS) at the universal tier of intervention. PW-PBIS is a framework for improving the learning environment, social-emotional skills of young children, and relationships among staff, families, and children in early childhood contexts (Fox & Hemmeter, 2009).

There are three proposed levels of intervention within PW-PBIS (Benedict et al., 2007; Stormont et al., 2005):

1. The universal level of prevention that is applied to all children in an early childhood program to prevent challenging behavior and social-emotional difficulties

2. The secondary level that involves intentionally teaching social-emotional, problem-solving, and friendship skills

3. The tertiary level of individualized and intensive function-based interventions for children who engage in severe and/or chronic challenging behavior

The PreSET measures the universal level of PW-PBIS as well as program-wide supports (e.g., administrator support of professional development, adequate time and resources) that are linked to successful adoption and sustainability of PW-PBIS over time.

HISTORY, RATIONALE, AND PROCEDURAL DETAILS

The PreSET is based on the School-Wide Evaluation Tool (SET; Sugai et al., 2001), an instrument used to measure fidelity of implementation of the universal level of SW-PBIS in K–12 school settings. The PreSET and SET share an overall purpose and have similar data collection procedures and organization and the same 3-point Likert scoring system. The SET is used widely in elementary, middle, and high schools across the nation, and it has established itself as a reliable and valid instrument to measure SW-PBIS implementation (Vincent et al., 2010).

Substantial revisions were made to language and content of SET items and subscales in order to yield an instrument that would fit the context of early childhood settings. For example, SET items that used language referring to rewards were removed or revised on the PreSET to focus on the use of praise and acknowledgment instead. The changed language fits with the more constructivist theoretical approach used by early childhood educators.

Two subscales that were not included in the SET—Organized and Predictable Environment and Family Involvement—were added to the PreSET. These subscales reflect the unique emphasis on classroom routines and family involvement in early childhood education. Furthermore, items and administration procedures across various subscales were revised on the PreSET to reflect the capabilities of toddler and preschool-age children. For example, during SET administration, the outside evaluator asks students about their school-wide behavioral expectations. During PreSET administration, however, the classroom teacher asks a sample of children, rather than the outside evaluator, about program-wide expectations. PreSET instructions prompt the teacher to use developmentally appropriate language to request this information (e.g., "What are our rules at school?") and to use visual or other adaptive language supports as necessary for children who are acquiring expressive language skills. The PreSET also acknowledges that specific curricula and strategies used as part of an early childhood program's implementation of PBIS should be age appropriate and are likely different than those used in SW-PBIS efforts.

The PreSET has been used in various research studies and as part of statewide PW-PBIS implementation since it was first developed in 2006. A preliminary analysis of the psychometric properties of scores on the PreSET is currently in preparation (Steed & Webb, under review). Specifically, the PreSET was used as a measure of preschool teachers' fidelity of implementation of classroom-level PBIS practices in four early childhood classrooms in the Pacific Northwest (Benedict et al., 2007) and in four preschool classrooms in the West (Carter & Van Norman, 2010). The PreSET administrator interview has also been used, in modified form, in a study assessing reported PBIS practices of approximately 45 early childhood staff including administrators, teachers, and behavior, family, and mental health specialists (Snell et al., in press). In practice, the PreSET has been used in statewide PW-PBIS implementation efforts in Oregon and New Hampshire and in local efforts in British Columbia, Nevada, and South Korea.

The PreSET includes 30 items that are divided into eight face-valid subscales that measure universal and program-wide features of PW-PBIS and, in large part, resemble those used in the SET. Six of the SET subscales (Expectations Defined, Expectations Taught, Responses to Appropriate and Challenging Behavior, Monitoring and Decision Making, Management, and Program Support) were adopted for use in the PreSET with relatively few changes. Specifically, select items from the SET subscales were modified (e.g., changed to fit language used in early childhood contexts) or removed to create an instrument that could be utilized in early childhood contexts. Two subscales were created, including Organized and Predictable Environment (five items) and Family Involvement (three items).

The PreSET takes approximately 1 hour to complete in a small early childhood program that includes one or two preschool classrooms, with an additional 20 minutes necessary for each additional classroom. Administration includes classroom observations of teacher behavior, review of permanent products, and interviews with the lead teacher, assistant teachers when applicable, a sample of children, and the early childhood program administrator. An outside evaluator completes the PreSET twice a year (once in the fall and once in the spring) during initial stages of PBIS implementation, moving to once a year after approximately 80% of PreSET items are in place.

To maintain consistency with the SET, each PreSET item is rated on a 3-point Likert scale with values ranging from 0 (not yet implemented), to 1 (partially implemented), or 2 (fully implemented). To preserve continuity with the scoring algorithm used in the SET, each subscale is scored by converting Likert ratings to a percentage correct score (i.e., the sum of Likert ratings is divided by the total possible sum—2 times the number of items—and multiplied by 100). Finally, a total score is computed by taking the mean percentage score of all eight subscales. In its current version, a PreSET score is determined after aggregating data from multiple classrooms from a preschool program on a single PreSET Scoring Guide. Previous PreSET administration instructions involved PreSET users scoring a PreSET Scoring Guide for each preschool classroom. At the time that these data were collected, the PreSET was being used as a classroom-level measure of fidelity of PBIS implementation and a PreSET Scoring Guide was completed for each classroom.

CHARACTERISTICS OF PARTICIPATING CLASSROOMS

The PreSET data included in this technical report included 138 early childhood classrooms: 101 in the Pacific Northwest, 31 in the southeastern United States, and 6 in the western United States. There were 66 Head Start classrooms, 26 private child care classrooms, 16 state-funded preschool classrooms, 15 special education classrooms, 11 public/nonprofit early childhood programs, and 4 preschool classrooms in an elementary school. In most cases (127 programs), an early childhood program provided PreSET data from a single classroom within its program. Eleven programs provided PreSET data from multiple classrooms (two or more) within their programs.

PSYCHOMETRIC PROPERTIES OF THE PreSET

This section presents descriptive statistics for PreSET items, subscales, and total scores as well as preliminary evidence of the reliability and validity of scores on the PreSET, including interobserver agreement, correlation of the PreSET with another widely used tool, and sensitivity of the PreSET to change.

Descriptive Statistics

The PreSET used for data analysis in this technical report includes 30 items that are organized into eight subscales: Expectations Defined, Expectations Taught, Responses to Appropriate and Challenging Behavior, Organized and Predictable Environment, Monitoring and Decision Making, Family Involvement, Management, and Program Support. Table C.1 provides a synopsis of the means, ranges, and standard deviations of items, subscales, and total PreSET scores. As a note of clarification, items are reported as scores on a 3-point Likert scale, subscales are reported as a percent score, and total scores represent the average percent obtained across the eight subscales.

In this sample, a range of values was observed across items, subscales, and total PreSET scores. In general, classrooms scored highest on items in the Organized and Predictable subscale, which also had the lowest variability of subscale scores. Classrooms scored lowest on items within the Management, Family Involvement, and Monitoring and Decision Making subscales (lowest to highest). Classrooms also performed lower compared to other items on Item 3 in the Expectations Taught subscale that related to children's ability to state the expectations for their classroom.

Correlations Among Subscales and Sampling Adequacy

Table C.2 summarizes item subscale, item total, and subscale total correlations as well as the internal consistency of each subscale. Item subscale correlations were reasonably strong with a mean of .56 and a median of .58. Item subscale correlations were stronger for some items (e.g., Management Items 1–4 were in the .82–.90 range, Expectations Defined Item 2 was .73, Monitoring and Decision Making Item 2 was .72) and more variable for others (e.g., Family Involvement Item 3 was .16, Responses to Appropriate and Challenging Behavior Item 1 was .23).

Item total correlations were also reasonably strong with a range from .12 to .75. Item total correlations were stronger for some items (e.g., Program Support Item 1 was .75, Expectations Defined Item 3 was .73) and more variable for others (e.g., Responses to Appropriate and Challenging Behavior Items 1 and 2 were .12 and .22, respectively). Each subscale total score was reasonably strong with a range from .39 to .71. The lowest

Table C.1.   PreSET item, subscale, and total score means, standard deviations (*SD*), and minimum and maximum scores (*n* = 138)

Subscale	Item	Mean	SD	Range
A: Expectations Defined		62.69	33.77	0–100
	1	1.51	0.79	0–2
	2	1.39	0.80	0–2
	3	0.86	0.95	0–2
B: Expectations Taught		59.74	35.99	0–100
	1	1.37	0.92	0–2
	2	1.39	0.82	0–2
	3	0.83	0.85	0–2
C: Responses to Appropriate and Challenging Behavior		64.20	26.63	0–100
	1	1.38	0.90	0–2
	2	1.38	0.93	0–2
	3	1.30	0.76	0–2
	4	1.36	0.94	0–2
	5	1.01	0.95	0–2
D: Organized and Predictable Environment		74.49	26.42	10–100
	1	1.37	0.84	0–2
	2	1.89	0.34	0–2
	3	1.29	0.87	0–2
	4	1.42	0.90	0–2
	5	1.48	0.88	0–2
E: Monitoring and Decision Making		42.28	37.03	0–100
	1	0.94	0.89	0–2
	2	0.93	1.00	0–2
	3	0.67	0.87	0–2
F: Family Involvement		38.86	31.49	0–100
	1	1.11	0.96	0–2
	2	0.70	0.80	0–2
	3	0.53	0.78	0–2
G: Management		33.91	40.93	0–100
	1	0.77	0.98	0–2
	2	0.66	0.88	0–2
	3	0.65	0.93	0–2
	4	0.83	0.97	0–2
	5	0.49	0.83	0–2
H: Program Support		57.58	41.21	0–100
	1	0.90	0.10	0–2
	2	1.29	0.95	0–2
	3	1.27	0.94	0–2
Total		53.86	24.73	2–99

performing subscale was Responses to Appropriate and Challenging Behavior (.39). This may be due to frequent instances in which classrooms received high scores in this subscale that focused on teacher–child interactions, use of praise, and consistent behavior management procedures while scoring low on program-wide practices related to data management, the presence of a leadership team, family involvement, and program support. This subscale may need improvement. Another low performing subscale was Family Involvement (.54). In this subscale, there was one item (Item 3) that had a low item subscale correlation (.16). This item also had the lowest mean score on Table C.1. This item may need to be revised. Across the eight subscales, there was an overall alpha of .91, demonstrating that the instrument as a whole demonstrates adequate internal consistency. The PreSET item,

Table C.2. PreSET item subscale, item total, and subscale total correlations and Cronbach α coefficients ($n = 138$)

Subscale	Item	$r_{i\text{-sub}}$	$r_{i\text{-tot}}$	$r_{sub\text{-tot}}$	α
A: Expectations Defined				.67	.80
	1	.66	.44		
	2	.73	.62		
	3	.57	.73		
B: Expectations Taught				.56	.78
	1	.64	.68		
	2	.58	.42		
	3	.63	.40		
C: Responses to Appropriate and Challenging Behavior				.39	.55
	1	.23	.12		
	2	.33	.22		
	3	.34	.36		
	4	.43	.41		
	5	.26	.25		
D: Organized and Predictable Environment				.59	.69
	1	.52	.57		
	2	.34	.24		
	3	.33	.35		
	4	.54	.44		
	5	.56	.50		
E: Monitoring and Decision Making				.71	.72
	1	.32	.49		
	2	.72	.64		
	3	.64	.62		
F: Family Involvement				.54	.59
	1	.53	.34		
	2	.58	.61		
	3	.16	.33		
G: Management				.52	.94
	1	.89	.57		
	2	.83	.61		
	3	.82	.53		
	4	.90	.62		
	5	.69	.64		
H: Program Support				.71	.82
	1	.71	.75		
	2	.64	.62		
	3	.65	.54		
Total					.91

subscale, and total score correlations met or exceeded recommendations for discriminability and internal consistency set at above .30 for item/scale correlations and .60 for total scores (Nunnally, 1975).

Given that the PreSET subscales were designed as components of the overall tool but also as unique scales within the tool, we anticipated positive correlations between all eight scales. As summarized in Table C.3, scales were moderately positively correlated with r ranging from .22 to .60 (median $r = .45$, mean $r = .42$). The Responses to Appropriate and

Table C.3.   PreSET subscale intercorrelations ($n = 138$)

Subscale	A	B	C	D	E	F	G	H
A: Expectations Defined	1.00	.56**	.37**	.45**	.56**	.40**	.45**	.51**
B: Expectations Taught		1.00	.33**	.49**	.32**	.54**	.22**	.48**
C: Responses to Behavior			1.00	.28**	.39**	.29**	.21*	.22*
D: Organized and Predictable Environment				1.00	.51**	.42**	.33**	.51**
E: Monitoring and Decision Making					1.00	.47**	.54**	.59**
F: Family Involvement						1.00	.22**	.46**
G: Management							1.00	.60**
H: Program Support								1.00

*$p < .05$. **$p < .01$.

Challenging Behavior subscale had the lowest correlations with other subscales. This is possibly due to its low alpha (.55). Furthermore, the Responses to Appropriate and Challenging Behavior subscale may be less conceptually related to fidelity of implementation of other features of PW-PBIS. In other words, teachers may receive high scores on this subscale due to their use of verbal praise and consistent behavior management strategies while receiving lower scores in other subscales, such as establishing and teaching expectations and using data management strategies.

A series of principal component and exploratory factor analyses were estimated to definitively test whether the eight subscales of the PreSET conformed to a single total score. The inspection of eigenvalues and a scree plot from the principal component indicated that a one-factor solution was optimal (eigenvalues = 4.0, 1.0, 0.8, 0.6, .0.6, 0.5, 0.3, 0.3). A single factor explained 50% of the observed variation in subscales. An exploratory factor analysis that forced one factor extraction yielded factor loadings greater than .40 for all eight PreSET scales (see Table C.4).

Consistent with the subscale-to-total correlations that were reported in Table C.2, the scales that contributed the most to the total score included Expectations Defined (factor loading = .73), Monitoring and Decision Making (factor loading = .75), and Program Support (factor loading = .76). Collectively, these results support the use of a total score from the PreSET. The Responses to Appropriate and Challenging Behavior subscale had the lowest factor loading as well as the lowest subscale to total correlation and alpha.

Interrater Reliability

Interobserver agreement was assessed on a subset of PreSET data ($n = 22$) in which two trained data collectors independently collected PreSET data in the same classroom. These 22 classrooms included 15 classrooms in the southeastern United States, 5 classrooms in the Pacific Northwest, and 2 classrooms in the western United States. There were 11 state-

Table C.4.   Factor loadings for exploratory factor analysis of eight subscales with one forced factor

Subscale	Factor
A: Expectations Defined	.73
B: Expectations Taught	.66
C: Responses to Appropriate and Challenging Behavior	.44
D: Organized and Predictable Environment	.65
E: Monitoring and Decision Making	.75
F: Family Involvement	.62
G: Management	.59
H: Program Support	.76
Total	.35

funded preschool classrooms, 7 private child care classrooms, 3 Head Start classrooms, and 1 special education classroom. In each administration of interrater reliability of the PreSET, one observer took the primary role of collecting data while a second observer collected data on a separate data sheet. Individuals who completed the PreSET were either SET trained or completed PreSET training with the first author of the tool. An agreement was scored when both observers scored the same response (0, 1, or 2) on each PreSET item. Percent agreement was calculated by dividing the number of agreements by the number of agreements plus disagreements. The average percent agreement on individual PreSET items was 95% with a range from 68% to 100%.

Given the high base rates of some items, we also computed coefficient κ values, which correct for chance agreement. Item κ scores ranged from 0 to 1.0, with the highest values observed for Expectations Defined Items 1 and 2, Monitoring and Decision Making Items 2 and 3, Family Involvement Items 1 and 2, Management Items 1–4, and Program Support Item 3. The lowest observed κ scores were for items in the Expectations Taught subscale. The overall κ was .80. Interrater agreement was high across PreSET item and total scores. Percent agreement and κ are reported on Table C.5.

Table C.5.   PreSET interobserver agreements and reliabilities (*n* = 22)

Subscale	Item	% agreement	κ
A: Expectations Defined	1	1.00	1.00
	2	1.00	1.00
	3	.95	.65
B: Expectations Taught	1	.91	.00
	2	.91	.47
	3	.91	.46
C: Responses to Appropriate and Challenging Behavior	1	.95	.88
	2	.91	.77
	3	.91	.84
	4	.95	.89
	5	.68	.52
D: Organized and Predictable Environment	1	.91	.86
	2	.86	.37
	3	.91	.78
	4	.91	.86
	5	.82	.69
E: Monitoring and Decision Making	1	.91	.83
	2	1.00	1.00
	3	1.00	1.00
F: Family Involvement	1	1.00	1.00
	2	1.00	1.00
	3	1.00	NA
G: Management	1	1.00	1.00
	2	1.00	1.00
	3	1.00	1.00
	4	1.00	1.00
	5	1.00	NA
H: Program Support	1	1.00	NA
	2	1.00	NA
	3	1.00	1.00
Average		.95	.80

Note: NA = Value could not be computed due to zero variance.

Construct Validity

To evaluate the construct validity of the PreSET, PreSET scores were correlated with scores from the Teaching Pyramid Observation Tool (TPOT; Fox et al., 2008), another measure used to assess fidelity of implementation of PBIS in early childhood classrooms. The TPOT measures all levels of PBIS, including universal, secondary, and individualized interventions for children with challenging behavior at the classroom level. Even though the PreSET measures only universal-level PBIS, the TPOT was the best instrument to use to measure construct validity. Both tools share the same overall purpose, to measure fidelity of implementation of PBIS in early childhood environments. The TPOT is frequently used as it is the only other measure for PBIS implementation in early childhood settings. It has demonstrated initial promise that it has strong psychometric properties (Hemmeter, Snyder, & Fox, 2010).

Although the two instruments share the same overall purpose, the PreSET and TPOT have divergent approaches to collecting and interpreting data and differences in the key features and items included on the assessments. The TPOT is exclusively used as a classroom-level assessment of teaching practices and environmental arrangements that are associated with positive social-emotional development in young children. The TPOT involves an interview with the lead teacher and a 2-hour observation of classroom practices across various routines that include circle time or small groups and free play or child-directed activities. A mix of scoring strategies is used to score the TPOT's 38 items. For example, Items 1–7 about the classroom environment and Items 23–38 about "red flags" are scored as *yes* or *no*, whereas Items 8–22 are scored as a percentage of indicators present. The PreSET was developed to address both classroom-level and program-wide implementation specifically at the universal level of PBIS. For this reason, we expected convergent validity on subscales in which the PreSET and TPOT have similarities (e.g., classroom environmental supports associated with the universal level of PBIS) and divergent validity related to constructs that are measured on only one of the tools (e.g., Monitoring and Decision Making is addressed on the PreSET but not the TPOT, Teaching Social Skills and Emotional Competencies is addressed on the TPOT but not on the PreSET).

We utilized a subset of the data ($n = 31$) where an external evaluator collected both PreSET and TPOT data in the same classroom. There were 16 state-funded preschool classrooms and 15 private childcare classrooms; all data were collected in the southeastern United States. Evaluators were trained to use the PreSET and TPOT by reviewing each instrument's manual and forms, reviewing the TPOT training podcast available online, and obtaining at least 85% reliability. PreSET and TPOT total scores from the 31 classrooms were modestly and positively correlated ($r = .33$). Table C.6 summarizes the correlations of PreSET and TPOT subscales that were expected to measure similar constructs and demonstrate higher correlations.

Scores on subscales that were conceptually linked between the PreSET and TPOT were modestly or moderately correlated. Examples included scores on the PreSET subscale Responses to Appropriate and Challenging Behavior that involves items related to teachers' use of praise and consistent behavior management strategies and the TPOT subscales Supportive Conversations ($.52, p < .01$) and Responding to Problem Behavior ($.58, p < .01$). Another example included scores on the PreSET subscale Organized and Predictable Environment that includes items related to the use of visual schedules and transition warnings and the TPOT subscales Classroom Environment ($.45, p < .05$), Schedules and Routines ($.52, p < .01$), and Transitions ($.55, p < .01$). Two PreSET subscales (Expectations Taught and Family Involvement) were positively correlated with their conceptual TPOT counterparts (Teaching Children Behavioral Expectations and Supporting Families' Social-Emotional Development), but the relationships were not statistically significant.

Table C.6.   PreSET and TPOT subscale and total correlations for subscales that were expected to be highly correlated (*n* = 31)

PreSET subscale	TPOT subscale(s)	Correlations
Expectations Defined	Teaching Children Behavior Expectations	.41*
Expectations Taught	Teaching Children Behavior Expectations	.25
Responses to Appropriate and Challenging Behavior	Supportive Conversations	.52**
	Responding to Problem Behavior	.58**
Organized and Predictable Environment	Classroom Environment	.45*
	Schedules and Routines	.52**
	Transitions	.55**
Family Involvement	Supporting Families' Social-Emotional Development	.19
Total	Total	.33

*$p < .05$; **$p < .01$.

As expected, scores on subscales that were not conceptually linked did not demonstrate significant positive correlations. An example is the low correlation of scores on the PreSET subscale of Monitoring and Decision Making with scores across TPOT subscales that ranged from –.31 to .19. This PreSET subscale includes items related to data collection procedures, data entry, and review of data for decisions about children's behavior intervention plans; this content is not included on the TPOT. Similarly, there were no significant correlations for scores on the PreSET subscale of Program Support and any of the TPOT subscales (–.33 to .29). Program support, including administrative support, planning time, resources, and professional development, are not measured by the TPOT. The results of these analyses demonstrate initial convergent validity for the PreSET as an instrument that measures fidelity of implementation of PBIS in early childhood settings with expected divergent validity from the TPOT on constructs in which the two tools differ in their focus.

Sensitivity to Change

Another strategy for evaluating the validity of the PreSET is to determine whether it is sensitive to detecting changes in a classroom or a center's implementation of PBIS strategies. To this end, pre- and postimplementation data were compared for 29 early childhood classrooms that were involved in training and coaching in PW-PBIS during the 2006–2007 academic year. Participating classrooms represented a range of early childhood settings, including half- and full-day Head Start, private and public preschool, and special education preschool classrooms. Three sets of two classrooms were located in the same building; all others were isolated classrooms in a preschool program; all classrooms were located in the Pacific Northwest. Following a fall PreSET evaluation conducted by a behavior specialist, all participating classroom teachers attended a 2-day training in PBIS and received individualized follow-up coaching. Behavior specialists had advanced training (e.g. master's degree) in early childhood special education or a related field and a teaching license in the state in which they worked. Information provided to teachers during training and consultation visits was derived from training modules by the Center on the Social and Emotional Foundations for Early Learning (2003). During consultation sessions, behavior specialists observed classroom practices and then facilitated discussion of teacher priorities for professional development, formation of goals for changes to the classroom environment (e.g., development and posting of a classroom rules poster) and/or teaching practices (e.g., use of more verbal praise), and follow-up during each visit on progress towards goals. Participating teachers received approximately 9.5 hours of consultation sessions across an

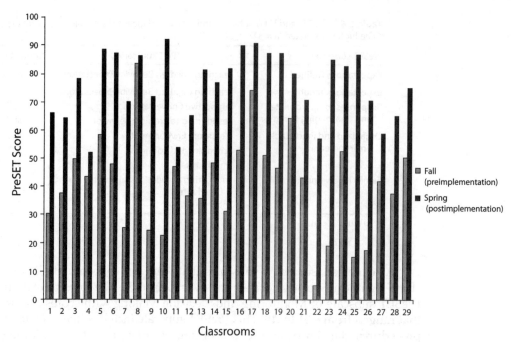

Figure C.1.   Mean pre- and postimplementation scores on the PreSET (*N* = 29).

average of nine classroom visits from behavior specialists. A spring PreSET evaluation was conducted in each classroom following the conclusion of consultation for the academic year.

Figure C.1 depicts the mean pre- and postimplementation PreSET total scores for each of the 29 classrooms. Preimplementation scores ranged from 5% to 84%, with a mean of 41%. Postimplementation scores ranged from 52% to 92%, with a mean of 76%. All of the classrooms showed an increase in their scores from fall to spring, as indicated by paired *t* tests (*t* = 10.49, *df* = 28, *p* < .000).

SUMMARY

1. The PreSET captures individual differences in PW-PBIS implementation.
2. The PreSET's eight face-valid subscales are correlated with each other in expected ways and, for most part, are internally consistent.
3. Exploratory factor analyses support the use of a total score.
4. Interrater reliability at the item level is acceptable.
5. The PreSET correlates with another measure of PBIS in early childhood settings.
6. The PreSET appears to be sensitive to change.

References

Benedict, E.A., Horner, R.H., & Squires, J. (2007). Assessment and implementation of positive behavior support in preschools. *Topics in Early Childhood Special Education, 27,* 174–192.

Blair, K.C., Fox, L., & Lentini, R. (2010). Use of positive behavior support to address the challenging behavior of young children within a community early childhood program. *Topics in Early Childhood Special Education, 30,* 68–79.

Carr, E.G., Dunlap, G., Horner, R.H., Koegel, R.L., Turnbull, A.P., Sailor, W., et al. (2002). Positive behavior support: Evolution of an applied science. *Journal of Positive Behavior Interventions, 4,* 4–16.

Carter, D.R., & Van Norman, R.K. (2010). Class-wide positive behavior support in preschool: Improving teacher implementation through consultation. *Early Childhood Education Journal, 38,* 279–288.

Center on the Social and Emotional Foundations for Early Learning. (2003). *Promoting the social emotional competence of young children: Training modules.* Nashville, TN: Vanderbilt University.

Cornely, P., & Bromet, E. (1986). Prevalence of behavior problems in three-year-old children living near Three Mile Island: A comparative analysis. *Journal of Child Psychology and Psychiatry, 27,* 489–498.

Duda, M.A., Dunlap, G., Fox, L., Lentini, R., & Clarke, S. (2004). An experimental evaluation of positive behavior support in a community preschool program. *Topics in Early Childhood Special Education, 24,* 143–155.

Dunlap, G., & Fox, L. (2009). Positive behavior support and early intervention. In W. Sailor, G. Dunlap, G. Sugai, & R. Horner (Eds.), *Handbook of positive behavior support* (pp. 49–72). New York: Springer.

Filter, K.J., McKenna, M.K., Benedict, E.A., Horner, R.H., Todd, A.W., & Watson, J. (2007). Check in/Check out: A post-hoc evaluation of an efficient, secondary-level targeted intervention for reducing problem behaviors in schools. *Education and Treatment of Children, 30,* 69–84.

Fox, L., Dunlap, G., Hemmeter, M.L., Joseph, G.E., & Strain, P.S. (2003). The Teaching Pyramid: A model for supporting social competence and preventing challenging behavior in young children. *Young Children, 58*(4), 48–52.

Fox, L., & Hemmeter, M.L. (2009). A program-wide model for supporting social emotional development and addressing challenging behavior in early childhood settings. In W. Sailor, G. Dunlap, G. Sugai, & R. Horner (Eds.), *Handbook of positive behavior support* (pp. 177–202). New York: Springer.

Fox, L., Hemmeter, M.L., & Snyder, P. (2008). *Teaching Pyramid Observation Tool for Preschool Classrooms (TPOT), Research Edition.* Unpublished assessment.

Fox, L., Hemmeter, M.L., Snyder, P., Binder, D.P., & Clarke, S. (2011). Coaching early childhood special educators to implement a comprehensive model for promoting young children's social competence. *Topics in Early Childhood Special Education, 31,* 178–192.

Frey, A.J., Park, K.L., Browne-Ferrigno, T., & Korfage, T.L. (2010). The social validity of program-wide positive behavior support. *Journal of Positive Behavior Interventions, 12,* 222–235.

Frey, A., Young, S., Gold, A., & Trevor, E. (2008). Utilizing a positive behavior support approach to achieve integrated mental health services. *HNHD: NHSA Dialog, 11,* 135–156.

Gilliam, W., & Shabar, G. (2006). Preschool and child care expulsion and suspension rates and predictors in one state. *Infants and Young Children, 19,* 228–245.

Green, B.L., Everhart, M., Gordon, L., & Gettman, M.G. (2006). Characteristics of effective mental health consultation in early childhood settings: Multilevel analysis of a national survey. *Topics in Early Childhood Special Education, 26,* 142–152.

Hawken, L., & Johnston, S. (2007). Preventing severe problem behavior in young children: The Behavior Education Program. *Journal of Early and Intensive Behavior Intervention, 4,* 599–613.

Hemmeter, M.L., Ostrosky, M., & Fox, L. (2006). Social emotional foundations for early learning: A conceptual model for intervention. *School Psychology Review, 35,* 583–601.

Hemmeter, M.L., Snyder, P., & Fox, L. (2010). *Examining the potential efficacy of a model for addressing social-emotional development and challenging behavior.* Presented at the Fifth Annual Institute of Education Sciences Research Conference, National Harbor, MD.

Horner, R.H., & Sugai, G. (2000). School-wide positive behavior support: An emerging initiative. *Journal of Positive Behavioral Interventions, 2,* 231–232.

Horner, R.H., Todd, A.W., Lewis-Palmer, T., Irvin, L.K., Sugai, G., & Boland, J.B. (2001). The School-Wide Evaluation Tool (SET): A research instrument for assessing school-wide positive behavior support. *Journal of Positive Behavior Interventions, 6,* 3–12.

Joseph, G.E., & Strain, P.S. (2008). *Early care providers' first responses to children's challenging behavior.* Paper presented at Division for Early Childhood Conference, Minneapolis, MN.

Kaiser, A.P., Cai, X., Hancock, T.B., & Foster, E.M. (2002). Teacher-reported behavior problems and language delays in boys and girls enrolled in Head Start. *Behavioral Disorders, 28,* 23–39.

Koegel, L.K., Koegel, R.L., & Dunlap, G. (1996). *Positive behavioral support: Including people with difficult behavior in the community.* Baltimore: Paul H. Brookes Publishing Co.

Muscott, H. and Pomerleau, T. (2008). *Challenging Behavior Definitions.* Bedford, NH: New Hampshire Center for Effective Behavioral Interventions and Supports.

New Hampshire Center for Effective Behavioral Interventions and Supports. (2009). *BIRS-NH Data Collection Form.* Bedford, NH: New Hampshire Center for Effective Behavioral Interventions and Supports.

New Hampshire Center for Effective Behavioral Interventions and Supports. (2009). *Behavior Incident Reporting System-NH.* Bedford, NH: New Hampshire Center for Effective Behavioral Interventions and Supports.

Nunnally, J.C. (1975). Psychometric theory 25 years ago and now. *Educational Researcher, 4,* 7-14, 14-20.

Patterson, G., Reid, J., & Dishion, T. (1992). *Antisocial boys.* Eugene, OR: Castalia Press.

Powell, D., & Dunlap, G. (2009). *Evidence-based social-emotional curricula and intervention packages for children 0–5 years and their families (Roadmap to Effective Intervention Practices).* Tampa, FL: University of South Florida, Technical Assistance Center on Social Emotional Intervention for Young Children.

Scott, T.M., Alter, P.J., Rosenberg, M., & Borgmeier, C. (2010). Decision-making in secondary and tertiary interventions of school-wide systems of positive behavior support. *Education and Treatment of Children, 33,* 513–535.

Snell, M.E., Stanton-Chapman, T.C., Voorhees, M.D., Berlin, R.A., Hadden, D.S., & McCarty, J.E. (in press). Reported practices of preschool staff concerning problem behavior and its prevention in Head Start classrooms: Implications for programs and in-service training. *Journal of Positive Behavior Interventions.*

Spaulding, S.A., Horner, R.H., May, S.L., & Vincent, C.G. (2008). *Implementation of school-wide PBIS across the United States. OSEP Technical Briefs.* Retrieved from http://www.pbis.org/evaluation/evaluation_briefs/nov_08_(2).aspx

Squires, J., Bricker, D., & Twombly, E. (2002). *Ages & Stages Questionnaires®: Social-Emotional (ASQ:SE): A Parent-Completed, Child-Monitoring System for Social-Emotional Behaviors.* Baltimore: Paul H. Brookes Publishing Co.

Steed, E.A. (2011). *Adapting the Behavior Education Program for preschool settings.* Manuscript submitted for publication.

Steed, E.A. (March, 2011). Assessing positive behavior support in childcare centers. *Association for Positive Behavior Support's 8th International Conference on Positive Behavior Support.* Denver, CO.

Steed, E.A., & Webb, M. (2011). *The Preschool-Wide Evaluation Tool: An instrument to measure program-wide positive behavior support in early childhood settings.* Manuscript submitted for publication.

Stormont, M., Lewis, T.J., & Beckner, R. (2005). Positive behavior support systems: Applying key features in preschool settings. *TEACHING Exceptional Children, 37*(6), 42–49.

Strain, P.S., Joseph, G.E., & Hemmeter, M.L. (2009). *Administrative practices that support fidelity implementation of the pyramid model.* Tampa, FL: Technical Assistance Center on Social Emotional Interventions, University of South Florida.

Sugai, G., & Horner, R. (2002). The evolution of discipline practices: School-wide positive behavior supports. *Child & Family Behavior Therapy, 24,* 23–50.

Sugai, G., Lewis-Palmer, T., Todd, A., & Horner, R.H. (2001). *School-wide evaluation tool.* Eugene: University of Oregon.

Technical Assistance Center on Social Emotional Intervention for Young Children (TACSEI). (2011). *Learn about the Pyramid Model*. Retrieved from http://www.challengingbehavior.org/do/pyramid_model.htm

Vincent, C., Spaulding, S., & Tobin, T.J. (2010). A reexamination of the psychometric properties of the School-Wide Evaluation Tool (SET). *Journal of Positive Behavior Interventions, 12,* 161–179.

Webster-Stratton, C. (2000). Oppositional-defiant and conduct disordered children. In M. Hersen & R. T. Ammerman (Eds.), *Advanced abnormal child psychology* (2nd ed., pp. 387–412). Mahwah, NJ: Lawrence Erlbaum Associates.

Wood, B., Blair, K.S., & Ferro, J. (2010). Young children with challenging behavior: Function-based assessment and intervention. *Topics in Early Childhood Special Education, 29,* 68–78.

References

Index

Page numbers followed by *f* and *t* indicate figures and tables, respectively.

Assess *program-wide* PBIS in early childhood with the complete PreSET™!

Preschool-Wide Evaluation Tool™ (PreSET™), *Research Edition*

Manual by Elizabeth A. Steed, Ph.D., & Tina M. Pomerleau, M.Ed.

Tool by Elizabeth A. Steed, Ph.D., Tina M. Pomerleau, M.Ed., & Robert H. Horner, Ph.D.

How well is your early childhood program implementing positive behavior intervention and supports (PBIS)? Find out with the complete PreSET™, a **manual** and comprehensive **tool on CD-ROM** that helps programs determine how well their interventions are working and what areas they need to work on.

Based on the widely used and highly regarded School-Wide Evaluation Tool (SET), PreSET™ assesses *program-wide* PBIS in all types of early childhood settings. Conducted twice a year by an unbiased outside observer—such as a behavioral consultant, inclusion coordinator, or school psychologist—PreSET™ takes an accurate snapshot of your program's PBIS through a review of **program documents, classroom observations,** and **interviews** with the administrator, teachers, and children from each classroom.

To implement PreSET™, your program needs:

▶ The **Manual** with thorough guidance on conducting and scoring PreSET™, a technical appendix of PreSET™ research, and a case study that walks the reader through an entire evaluation.

▶ The **CD-ROM** with all the printable forms: the four PreSET™ forms (Administrator Interview, Classroom Interview and Observation, Classroom Summary, and Scoring Guide), plus two forms for planning next steps (Action Plan and Feedback Form).

With this comprehensive tool, you'll have the data you need to determine how well PBIS is working, target interventions and program improvements, and work toward better social-emotional development for all young children.

Use PreSET™ to help your program

▶ Assess universal features of effective PBIS, including behavioral expectations, family involvement, and program support

▶ Take first steps toward improving the social-emotional skills children need for kindergarten

▶ Measure progress toward goals

▶ Work on trouble spots so you can report better outcomes to OSEP

▶ Target quality improvement efforts

▶ Determine teacher professional development needs

Purchase both the manual and the tool for accurate implementation:

MANUAL—US$50.00 • Stock Number: BA-72070
2012 • 136 pages • 8 ½ x 11 • paperback
ISBN 978-1-59857-207-0

TOOL—US$99.95 • Stock Number: BA-72087
2012 • 34 pages on CD-ROM
ISBN 978-1-59857-208-7

Training available through Brookes On Location! See www.brookesonlocation.com